ONE CHANCE

Owen Joshua Lewsey was born in 1976 in England, from Welsh blood. As well as being one of the world's best rugby players and a test British Lion, he holds a Physiology degree from Bristol University, a postgraduate degree in Law and has served as a commissioned officer in the British Army. He left the military in 2002 to concentrate wholly on rugby, and was awarded an MBE one year later for his role in the triumphant 2003 World Cup. He retired from both club and international rugby in 2009.

D1382005

ONE CHANCE

My Life and Rugby

Josh Lewsey

Published by Virgin Books 2010

2 4 6 8 10 9 7 5 3

Copyright © Josh Lewsey 2009

Statistics compiled by Stuart Farmer

Josh Lewsey has asserted his right under the Copyright, Designs and Patents Act 1988
to be identified as the author of this work

This book is sold subject to the condition that it shall not, by way of trade or otherwise,
be lent, resold, hired out, or otherwise circulated without the publisher's prior consent
in any form of binding or cover other than that in which it is published and without a
similar condition, including this condition, being imposed on the subsequent purchaser.

Every reasonable effort has been made to contact copyright holders of material reproduced
in this book. If any have inadvertently been overlooked the publishers would be glad to hear
from them and make good in future editions any errors or omissions brought to their
attention.

First published in Great Britain in 2009 by
Virgin Books
Random House, 20 Vauxhall Bridge Road,
London SW1V 2SA

www.virginbooks.com
www.rbooks.co.uk

Addresses for companies within The Random House Group Limited can be found at:
www.randomhouse.co.uk/offices.htm

The Random House Group Limited Reg. No. 954009

A CIP catalogue record for this book is available from the British Library

ISBN 9780753515570

The Random House Group Limited supports The Forest Stewardship Council [FSC], the
leading international forest certification organisation. All our titles that are printed on
Greenpeace approved FSC certified paper carry the FSC logo.
Our paper procurement policy can be found at www.rbooks.co.uk/environment

Mixed Sources
Product group from well-managed
forests and other controlled sources
www.fsc.org Cert no. TT-COC-2139
© 1996 Forest Stewardship Council

Typeset by TW Typesetting, Plymouth, Devon
Printed and bound in Great Britain by CPI Bookmarque Ltd, Croydon CR0 4TD

Talent is not enough. You must have the right mindset. To get to the top and stay there you have to want to be the best in the world with every ounce of your mind, body and soul. You have to make great sacrifices. You must throw yourself into new experiences to learn and improve continuously in order to develop and hone your skills so that they become second nature. You must make the right decisions on and off the park; and you must not upset anyone important, even if they deserve it.

If you can do all this, then you will have the confidence to trust yourself. This will free your mind to let your talents flow and luck will help you on your way.

Richard Rivett

This book is dedicated to all the Richard Rivetts, the John Williams, the Dick Davies, the Ross Panters, Roy Jarolds, and David and Mair Lewseys out there – the parents, teachers and volunteers who willingly give up their own time to inspire, enthuse, motivate and mentor young people. You are the grass-roots of every sport and the fabric of communities, but what's more, you have the power to change lives and fulfil dreams.

CONTENTS

Introduction

Given that this is an autobiography, it may sound bizarre to state that I've written this book myself. This isn't a boast, or an apology, but merely to say that I have not, as is often the case with sports biographies, used a ghostwriter. To that end I stand accountable for my thoughts, opinions and views.

Therefore, I hope those who read this will take what I say in the context of how I mean it, which is usually with fond affection. Of course, I'm not always right and, reading this years from now, I may be proved wrong in various areas, but I've given my opinions and version of events as I saw them, straightforwardly and honestly.

Such honesty has at times ruffled feathers, even got me into trouble, but I'd like to think that at least I have always been myself and genuine with those around me.

Writing the book has been an enormously enjoyable and in many ways cathartic experience but the biggest challenges have been:

1. Striking the delicate balance between speaking the truth in an even and fair way, being honest in my own opinions and yet not wishing to be deliberately controversial or offensive to others.

2. Making those funny times I reminisce about seem funny to you, the reader, who wasn't actually there, and who doesn't have an intimate knowledge of the characters involved.
3. Giving an intimate description of people's characters without breaking their confidence and, more importantly, maintaining loyalty towards them.
4. Spelling!

Last but not least, I see myself as having been exceptionally fortunate to get paid for doing something I simply love. I have written this book as a keepsake of my life and career to date but, most importantly, hope to share some of the wonderful times that I've had living it. I hope you enjoy it too.

Yours,
Josh
November 2008.

Chapter 1

Scallywags

IT SEEMS TO BE accepted practice in the world of sporting autobiographies to start with one's childhood, accompanied by some rather gawky pictures at school, a team photo and the obligatory bad haircut, and to give a chronological account from there. So, in time-honoured tradition, that's how I'll begin.

My childhood was, on the whole, not that much different from anyone else's. I was born in Bromley, south-east London, in 1976, the middle child of three boys. I have no affiliation to the place of my birth because we moved to the more homely and comfortable surroundings of rural Norfolk while I was still very young. Having two academic parents, both of them with Welsh roots (my mum, Mair, is Welsh, my dad, David, half-Welsh, half-English), meant that many summers were spent crossing the country and travelling down the M4 towards South Wales, spending time playing in the pools, streams and tributaries of the Twrch, and eating vast quantities of *bara brith* (Welsh fruitcake). Mamgu (Elunid), our grandmother, was an angel of a woman who took huge delight in filling our young bellies with lovingly prepared home-cooked food.

Dadgu (Emrys), my mother's father, was captain and fly half of Ystalyfera and, though ill with emphysema – he had worked in the pits from the age of twelve – and, by the time we got to know him properly, Alzheimer's, he remained a respected and well-liked man in the local community. It was this link with Wales that perhaps had the most influence on me and my brothers, Tom and Edward. Having been born in the mid-seventies during the time of The King – Barry John – and other Welsh greats like Gareth Edwards, we were more than a little conscious that rugby was the national pastime in the principality. All three Lewsey boys were to dream of playing the pivotal role of halfback in the magic red jersey of Wales.

Having come from mining stock in Cwmllynfell on the edge of the Black Mountains, my mother was keen to see life outside her close-knit community and left home to study history at Aberystwyth University. Dad was reading physics there and the 'romantic' tale of how they met has gone down in family lore. Playing in the university rugby team in the days when the opposition used to stay overnight, Dad challenged his opposite number to a drinking contest. Having lost, he proceeded to throw up into the lap of the nearest woman, an attractive brunette. Understandably somewhat put out, she didn't speak to him for two years. Some years later, the pair now happily married, Thomas Rhys – Tom – was born, the first of three boys who would carry on in the same genteel manner!

Two years after Tom was born, I came along, and then in 1979 Edward was born. We were still in London at this point, and my poor mother still recalls being dragged around countless rugby grounds as Dad turned out for Old Colfeians! By the late seventies the family moved to the historic city of Norwich in East Anglia, and that's where my first memories begin. It was a happy time. I enjoyed school and fairly quickly we three boys established ourselves in the local 'close'.

Mum was teaching history at secondary school, and Dad was working as sales director at IBM in Norwich. I remember Dad bringing home a computer one day. The fact that it was about the size of a house didn't diminish our excitement, but then, typical males through and through, we quickly grew bored when we couldn't work out how to use it, having already thrown away the instructions. I remember, too, Tom getting his first bicycle without stabilisers. The first bike is a big moment in any child's life but that was almost overshadowed by Edward's and my amusement as we tried to jab a stick between the spokes as Tom rode it!

That bike taught us the importance of not being too image-conscious or obsessed with brands. In hindsight, we tried to generate our own values about what really mattered in life. In those days toys weren't quite what they are nowadays and, thanks to some pretty robust treatment, the bike didn't stay in one piece for long. Not to worry, though. Grandpa – Dad's father, who lived in Royston – was a genius at making things; he was the DIY equivalent of Ray Mears. Hardly a Christmas went by when we didn't get a home-made castle, or a go-cart. Don't get me wrong: I'm not exactly obsessed about such things but in today's health-and-safety-conscious world the sharpened metal watchtowers and turrets or the deregulated attached air rifle would not have got production approval on a commercial level, though even back then their suitability for clumsy small boys might have been stretching it!

Despite Grandpa clearly disliking us, preferring instead to shut himself in the garage and smoke rather than having us hanging around, irritating him, I remember thinking he was pretty cool. He once gave me neat gin instead of water when I ran in thirsty from playing football, and roared with laughter as I cried and my throat burned. Grandpa was only too happy when he was scouring skips and rubbish tips for any odds and sods that could be made useful, and that meant that this former company quartermaster sergeant thought nothing of welding a BMX front to a Raleigh racer back to 'make do'. Other kids didn't see it quite like that; they were more preoccupied with the make of the bike than who actually won the races, not missing the opportunity to tease Tom when his bike came apart at the welded joints when he was trying some stunts. Rather embarrassed, Tom responded in the eloquent and intellectual manner that being part of a competitive trio had taught him: he left two older kids bleeding in the street . . . bless him!

This 'make do and mend' attitude continued throughout my school career. At Watford Grammar School, as senior prefect, I like to think I would have set a good example with the support of my peers, and commanded some respect. Yet, despite being the only family with a tennis court and a seven-bedroom house, we all individually at some stage developed the nickname of 'gypo'. This nickname could have stemmed from our reluctance to adopt airs and graces and our grounded mentality, but it probably came about because we boys drove a clapped-out Metro without a dashboard that was so crap even the kids on benefit took the piss. It was this ability not to take ourselves too seriously, to establish our own values of what mattered in life and respect achievement that, I believe, made us all the independent, self-reliant characters we are today.

People often ask me how old I was when I started playing rugby. The answer is four. Usually you're not allowed to start playing until the age of six, but once they'd dropped us off at the club in the morning, and we ran around for free and came home knackered and ready for bed, I think Mum and Dad quickly came to see rugby as a cheap form of babysitting! Of course we all loved it; it was a cracking way for energetic youngsters to learn some very good social, moral and physical skills. I was a very small but pretty nippy mop of blond hair and I realised fairly early on that if you wanted to stop someone bigger than yourself you had to even up the odds. Short of kicking them in the goolies, the next best thing was to go for their lowest point – their ankles. At the time I remember being taught that saving a try was as important as, if not better than, scoring one, a lesson that some of the headline-seeking youngsters now playing the professional game would do well to learn.

The club I played for was North Walsham, set in a rural part of Norfolk, so there were a lot of farmers' boys in the team – easily identified by the elongated arms they acquired through a life of loading bales of hay and shifting pigs. Most notable was a boy called Joe Beardshaw. I have a picture at home of me and Joe in our first week of club rugby and I'm delighted to say that we eventually played again together for Wasps and are still good friends to this day. And – sorry, Joe – he is still called Monkey because his arms are so long!

When I was six we left Norfolk for Hertfordshire. We'd bought a big house in a pretty hamlet between the villages of Sarratt and Chipperfield. The school I went to was Sarratt JMI, about a mile's walk from home or a few minutes by car for Mum on her way to work. Despite us moving into an area where to me everyone seemed to sniff a lot and had funny accents – compared to my East Anglian twang they sounded like characters from a Dickens novel – we all settled in fairly quickly. Chris Alexander was the headmaster of Sarratt JMI; he was a firm but kind man with a passion for sport. I remember playing enormous amounts of all sports in those days, running around every playtime and generally loving being outside. I have kept my love of open spaces to this day, still enjoying outdoor activities. One thing that also became clear – even though I probably didn't realise it at the time – was that Grandpa was basically a countryman, bright, and a phenomenal font of knowledge about wildlife, especially birds. Often perceived as awkward, he was, on reflection, more shy than difficult; and having once been a gamekeeper, he understood the delicate balance between life and death and was always more comfortable in the simple presence of God's creatures than in the incessant noise of modern humanity. Similarities between us haven't gone unremarked!

As I have mentioned, we spent countless hours outside playing all types of sport and when at home used up every spare moment hitting each other with tennis rackets or ruining Mum's beautifully tended garden playing games. Being open-minded and ambitious for us, my parents wanted us to diversify our interests and tried hard to get us interested in more subtle and refined pastimes. Hence the obligatory piano and violin lessons; we also took drama at school and I distinctly remember being taken to see *Swan Lake* at the local theatre. But without being snobby, *Swan Lake* at Watersmeet, Rickmansworth, is somewhat different to the Royal Opera House, and so it didn't quite have the desired impact. They obviously failed miserably in their efforts to get us interested in other things at the time: beating each other up was still what we did best. They did, though, manage to instil a certain balance in our characters; although none of us is particularly gifted in other areas, we all now respect and appreciate the fact that there's more to life than rugby. Mum achieved this – whether by cunning, wit or just sheer desperation is open to debate – and certainly succeeded in stopping us talking about nothing but rugby. Sunday was rugby day up at our junior club, Amersham & Chiltern. We all played for our respective age groups, Tom for the Under 9s, me for the Under 7s and Edward with the little ones, and after *Rugby Special* and *Ski Sunday* we'd sit down for the Sunday meal. Bless Mum. I'm sure she yearned for some female company and was desperate to listen to more than the usual recitation of who scored what and who won. Eventually she declared that she'd had enough: 'Right then, I'm fed up with bloody rugby. It's all you talk about. From now on if anyone mentions it during Sunday meals, you won't get pudding.' Now bearing in mind that there was jam roly-poly or spotted dick and custard at stake, Sunday meals didn't involve much talking after that.

It is my biggest regret that I gave up on music, as I'm now enormously envious of anyone who can play a musical instrument. My good friend Jon 'Fingers' Lacey is always a hit at all sorts of gatherings and his presence alone at the keyboard is enough to guarantee a good night. In fact, my brother Edward has now taught himself to play again in his TV-less house in Exeter; specialising in the music of Welsh folk singers Dafydd Iwan and Max Boyce, he also pulls off a rather rousing version of 'You Are My Sunshine' for Grandma's old people's home.

Tom was exceptionally bright academically and won a scholarship to a local private school, Haberdashers' Aske's, Elstree. However, having spent his childhood playing poker – his father, amongst his other talents, had been a professional gambler for a while – Dad wasn't one to miss a trick. At the time, Sarratt JMI was a feeder for the local comprehensive, with no one going on to the highly rated Watford Boys Grammar School. It was then and still is one of the best grammar schools in the country but, being outside its catchment area, we'd have been unlikely to get in. The school had an automatic entrance policy for siblings and so, armed with the offer of an academic scholarship from the local top-rated private school, Dad made a point of choosing Watford for Tom instead. It was only later that he said, 'Oh, didn't I mention there are two more?'

By then differences began to emerge between Tom, Edward and me. It's not surprising that, like most siblings, we were reasonably competitive, not just in sports but also in the puzzles and board games we played regularly on a Sunday night. Living in Thatcher's Britain as we were at the time, the good old capitalist values of greed and competition were encouraged, and Monopoly was the board game that encapsulated the spirit of the moment. Edward, being five years old, was sent to bed after being made bankrupt by landing on Dad's Mayfair. After an hour of tears he still refused to go to sleep and, exhausted, with school the next day, Mum pleaded his case to come back and join the game. But Dad was adamant: 'Mair, he's got to learn!'

We were also very fortunate to travel so much. Mum and Dad believed in showing us different cultures and though the holiday homes of south-west England or the sunshine of the Costa del Crime may have been infinitely more convenient, the lure of 'adventure' and the challenge and fun of trying to speak the language, even though we couldn't, were considerably more appealing. We were financially quite comfortable and yet, despite being relatively spoiled with such holiday destinations, if there was an opportunity to create stress or to bend the rules then we'd take it. Hitch-hiking around Greece springs to mind, staying in bug-infested youth hostels, having to pretend we were eight to get on rides cheaper – even when I was twelve – and bypassing border guards in Calais at 60mph to catch the ferry. Any whingeing got a swift response: 'You're not here to enjoy yourselves, you're here to make the most of it.'

We were also lucky enough to ski a fair bit, often sharing family holidays with our friends the Toulsons. Mr Toulson, Alan, was a senior partner in a law firm, and a captain of industry; Sarah, his wife, was the typical English rose. Their son, Luke, was a great mate of mine and along with Bonny, Katie and Sam they made up the most lovely, affectionate family you could think of. We complemented them. Anyone who has skied the slopes of the French Alps will know how ridiculously expensive food and drink can be in the mountain cafés. Usually staying half board, and having fairly healthy metabolisms, it didn't take long for us to work out who wasn't eating their lunch properly. While Luke, Bonny and co. were tucking into their lunchtime croque-monsieurs and chocolat chauds, we were encouraged to 'fill our boots' at breakfast and last through the day. Starving by lunchtime, we'd send Edward, 'the nice one', to chat up older, lonely French girls, more concerned about their weight than talking to boys aged six, eight and ten. Tom would work the left flank and I'd pick off their mates.

I also loved going down to Wales. Dad's family, rehoused there during the war, was predominantly from north Hertfordshire and, as an only child, he didn't have much close family. Mum, on the other hand, from your typical Welsh mining village, had lots of aunties, uncles and cousins. They were all lovely to us and I for one was happiest there, with a special fondness for her mother, Mamgu. Even when I was naughty as a little boy or a difficult and unruly teenager, she was always kind and scrupulously fair. As I've said, she fed us huge amounts of food, and I remember her once saying to my best friend who, bloated after an enormous meal she'd prepared, had declined any more: 'Wash it down with some trifle.'

Alun, my uncle, was also a very sweet man whose generosity knew no bounds. In such a small community, after retirement he regularly won competitions for his vegetable garden and thought nothing of giving all the produce to neighbours and relatives, never accepting a penny. I remember him taking me to Stradey Park, the home of Llanelli, and watching my cousin Ian Davies play for arch-rivals Swansea. On the way to the match he taught us the words of 'Sospan Vach', the famous club anthem. I think it was my first proper game of rugby and frankly I loved it. Alun had spent every day of his working life, as his father had, in the mines and most notably on the 'breaker'. Think of the machinery road builders use to dig up the roads and you'll know what I mean. Having done a couple of days' ball-breaking work either on building sites or on my own house using one of these, all I can say is that to do forty-two years on the breaker without a murmur or whinge – he's a tougher man than I am.

* * *

The eighties was a difficult time for South Wales. The reper-cussions of the pit closures in the mid-eighties were still being felt in men's social clubs, the emergence of the supermarkets was squeezing the farming industry and that source of national happiness and pride – the Welsh rugby team – wasn't successful either, losing many of its best players to the lure of professional rugby league. It is therefore with great delight that I've watched their recent success – notably the 2008 Grand Slam – under the management of Warren Gatland and Shaun Edwards. I know how much it means to them.

The clash of culture and wealth between Cwmllynfell and the comparatively opulent if disengaged surroundings of the leafy Home Counties was, on reflection, startling. Such polar opposites did, though, I'd like to think anyway, give us a rounded view of people. I can understand why some people from the Celtic countries dislike the English, labelling them (incorrectly most of the time) as pompous snobs or Hooray Henrys. Conversely, when I hear the odd idiot arrogantly lambasting them in turn, saying that the only problem with Monmouthshire is that it's full of Welsh, it makes my blood boil.

Chapter 2

Rugby First

M Y HAPPIEST MEMORIES of childhood are of days spent up at
Amersham & Chiltern RFC from the early eighties, when I
was six or seven, to about 1994. I'd found something I was good
at, and our coaches Dick Davies and Richard Rivett encouraged a
running style of play that got us all participating. The sports clubs
around the country, their success and level of participation depend
entirely upon the goodwill, enthusiasm, hard work and dedication
of the many volunteers and parents who give up their spare time,
and we were lucky in Amersham & Chiltern to have that in
spades. Both Dick and Richard were fathers of lads in the team:
Joe Davies, our lighthouse of a second row, being a farmer's boy
supplying pork to Waitrose, went on to qualify as a vet, and James
Rivett, a confrontational prop, is now a successful City banker.

For my entire youth I played fly half – the decision-maker, the
caller of moves – and with a fairly nifty sidestep and turn of speed
managed to run in a few tries too. I coach children on many
occasions nowadays and try to get up to Amersham & Chiltern,
where the rugby bug first bit me, as often as possible. Even at such

an early age, I still think it's possible to spot the ones with real, natural ability. As far as scouting goes, I'm led to believe that most professional sports look first for athleticism, believing that you can teach skills for a particular sport later. I don't necessarily agree with this philosophy; with the right training programme anyone can become fit and strong but the inherent knowledge of what to do at a particular time, an understanding of the game and how to use those around you to manipulate space are much more important than how much you bench. Of course, in order to achieve at any level, technique doesn't work without the requisite horsepower, but if someone is both a natural footballer and a good athlete he just needs the right mental faculties to reach international level. But at a pre-pubescent age fitness and size are less of an issue, and in my dubbined-up pair of steel-toed, high-cuts I'm told I looked a worthy opponent. What Richard Rivett saw in me was that I was clearly a very good player who could win games single-handed. In fact, though I could often run the length of the pitch by myself, I was always encouraged to involve others, being given a Mars bar or similar treat when I set up a try for someone else – conditioned like Pavlov's dog.

We had great sides in all age groups, and being based in an affluent area of south Buckinghamshire, where aspiring schools gave the boys rugby four times a week, we competed and won most of the time. Nick Bottomley was scrum half, but once he rightly saw sense and found a more interesting pastime – girls – he was replaced by a typically tenacious Scot, Martin Smith. Michael Parsons played centre and, being fiery, powerful and quick, tore up most midfields. My good mate from school Braden Dunsmore, 'the tackler', played outside, with the elusive pace of Charlie Hutchins on the wing. Charlie's family was charismatic, especially his father, John, who was always very kind to me. With his shooting stick he'd follow the team faithfully around various tournaments and competitions. It always amused us that, even as a boy, Charlie was made to wear a tweed jacket and tie after games, especially as the rest of us were usually in too much of a hurry to pinch the penny sweets to even bother washing.

More than anything else it was the feeling that I was special, that I was valued at something, which made me most content. At the time Dad was coach of Edward's team, and as he was probably their best player Dad wasn't going to leave home without him. Edward quickly realised this and, being the baby of the family and happy-go-lucky by nature, it meant hours waiting for him to get ready. My spies in Exeter, where he now plays and teaches, tell me nothing's changed! Tom and I, on the other hand, were dropped all around the country in lay-bys and service stations and given grid references for poor old Richard and Roy Jarold, Tom's coach, to drive out of their way to pick us up.

Mum, after a week's hard graft at the local school teaching history to pimply adolescents, would, like all the mothers, roll up her sleeves and help in the kitchen preparing bacon butties and hot dogs. It is volunteers like Mum who deserve all the accolades: they provide the cornerstone not just of rugby but of all grass-roots sport in this country and, what's more, create a healthy community in doing so.

I loved Sundays so much during the rugby season and frankly got bored stiff in the off season. Mum and Dad tried in vain on numerous occasions to punish me if I was naughty. 'Grounded' wasn't an issue – we lived seven miles from my nearest mates. 'Stop pocket money' didn't work either as I hadn't discovered girls yet and thus had nothing to spend it on except sweets, in which case I'd just pinch the second layer of chocolates from the box Mum kept for the next dinner party (we all became fairly adept at resealing any opened food container!). But when on one occasion I wasn't allowed to go to rugby, Dad driving off leaving me practically in tears, I cycled up there anyway. Bearing in mind it's a twelve-mile hike over the Chilterns I wasn't exactly on top form that day.

At primary school we had played all sports, but I particularly excelled at football. At the age of eleven, when I was just about to start at Watford Boys Grammar School, I had to make the choice between football and rugby. To be truthful I was probably better at football than rugby, having captained Watford District when I was ten, and was asked if I would consider an apprenticeship with a few of the big First Division clubs – this was before the Premier League. Although the thought of playing computer games and doing only remedial reading and writing sounded fun, football wages hadn't reached the stratospheric levels of today and thus the more traditional school route was chosen. Going to a grammar school that prided itself on rubbing shoulders with the great and the good, we played rugby, hockey and cricket but, as anyone who knows me will tell you now, I haven't played the last two since those days.

I found school enormously exciting. Watford Boys Grammar School punches above its weight and, along with its sister school, regularly excels in those questionable and debatable academic league tables. It's true what they say about everyone remembering a good teacher and there were certainly plenty to pick from, and not just in terms of academic lessons: the school had a very good reputation for its broad extracurricular activities. The year I joined, 1988, David Pyatt won the Young Musician of the Year award, and during my time we twice won the *Observer* Mace competition for debating. There was a full arts and drama itinerary of events and, of course, sport in all forms was actively encouraged.

These days I have an ongoing, good-humoured debate with Fraser Waters, my old Bristol University and Wasps colleague, about where we'd send our children. He was educated at Harrow – a school whose prestige, heritage, political influence and number of British prime ministers it has produced would be hard to match. But as essentially a comprehensive school at the time, based in a culturally diverse area of Watford, and therefore obliged to take a quota of local entrants, WBGS represented better, I feel, the broad spectrum of society. And so, not being a 'narrow-minded bubble-boy bigot', and having grown up with the sons of parents from various professions and backgrounds, I reckon it kept me and my brothers grounded and made us more determined than ever.

Academically I was competent enough but I was never one to breeze through without effort. Sciences and maths resonated with me far more than languages, and to this day my spelling is so awful that even as I type this with the spell-check turned on, the computer struggles to recognise certain words. At the time I thought French would be a useful language to learn, what with the various holidays we had. After a few minor rearrangements I found myself in the same set as those whose first language wasn't even English! Geography was fun; in its most basic form it seemed that a pass mark would be achieved by colouring in the right bits blue, green or brown. To this day I still regret that you couldn't do both history and geography for GCSE; they would definitely have given me more chance of doing well than boring old English Lit. With a history graduate for a mother and a younger brother who would later pursue it into teaching, I enjoyed the political elements of it, having been lectured on pretty much every car journey we ever took. Trips to Bath covered the quarrying of stone, Wales and further north the Industrial Revolution, France the two world wars, NATO and communism, Stonehenge the ancient Britons – which led on to the Romans, the Norman/Saxon squabbles, coming back of course to the persecution of the Celtic races at the hands of the English, and so on.

It was sport, however, that defined me. Sport was something I was really good at and the source of any confidence and self-identity I had. But I had begun to drift. Being a slow developer physically I could no longer rely purely on natural ability. I'd never lost a running race until I was thirteen but seemingly overnight the boys I went to school with had suddenly grown into men and I hadn't even started. The opportunity to excel at anything was suddenly being taken away from me. I began to feel very frustrated with rugby and, though still more than capable, perhaps began to lose my way a little. At that time the key phrase in the English game was 'percentage rugby'. The crowd seemed to cheer most when the ball bounced into touch. Fly halves were picked for their kicking ability and if the ball ever went beyond the inside centre something had gone wrong. In short, the game bored me, and I wasn't suited to this new style. I'd grown up wanting to be Jonathan Davies, not Naas Botha or Rob Andrew. I was excited by the likes of Jeremy Guscott, Ieuan Evans and Serge Blanco, not some war of attrition in the mud. Of course, in the modern era winning is what counts – and rightly so – but the best teams have always been able to mix and match accordingly, getting the right balance at the right time, blending sheer pragmatism with aesthetic pleasure.

I remember watching Andy Harriman and Everton Davies scoring tries for fun at the Middlesex Sevens every year and being thrilled. (Despite Sevens being overlooked in the professional age it is still one of my proudest achievements that in 2006, with eleven, I broke the record for the number of tries scored in that tournament.) Dad took me down to Cardiff Arms Park for my first international, when Wales beat Scotland in their Triple Crown year of 1989. Jonathan Davies scored 'a mesmeric try' – and Ieuan Evans sidestepped their whole team to score the most amazing try – 'Merlin the magician couldn't have done it any better'. I was overcome with the emotion of it all: this was what I wanted. As you can see I even memorised Bill McLaren's commentary of those tries, but English rugby seemed to have no place for an idealistic pre-pubescent teenager who wouldn't kick.

Unsurprisingly, at what is a difficult period in most people's lives, my disillusionment spilled over into other areas. Relationships in an already competitive, male-dominated household became fraught and I always felt socially awkward. I was lacking direction, got in fights all the time, and found myself detached, misunderstood and unhappy.

Cue the intervention of a brilliant and kind man, Richard Rivett. Richard, you'll remember, was our coach at Amersham & Chiltern and he perhaps understood me better than I did myself. He pulled me aside and gave me some advice that, arguably, changed my life. Essentially, he told me straight that my talent and ability were rare, but without matching them with equal measures of desire and determination it would all be wasted (see page v of this book). Wasting opportunities and potential was what average people did.

Whether or not I would eventually have sussed that out by myself I will never know, but I look back to that point in my life and, without wishing to embarrass him, see it as a milestone. Everyone needs a Richard Rivett, and I consider myself enormously lucky to have been given that advice at that time. Without getting too sentimental about it, I do believe that many of the issues that today's youngsters face could be overcome if they had a similar mentor or could just find a direction into which to channel their energies.

After our chat, not without a little reflection on my part, I quickly went to work. Initially my focus was purely on sport. I had a huge interest in physiological sciences and started working hard on my fitness. At the time I desperately tried to get hold of some decent training routines and learn more about the science of training. What type of training would make you quicker? What did I need to do to get stronger and better aerobically? At the time there wasn't even a gym at the school and, as such, in an age of characters such as Sly Stallone's Rocky Balboa and his nemesis Ivan Drago, and one of my all-time sporting heroes, the boxer

Nigel Benn, I saved my pocket money and bought a cheap punching bag from Argos. As he went to school in north London, Nigel Benn was considered a local lad. He was nicknamed 'The Dark Destroyer', having won all the boxing weight belts during his army career with the First Battalion, The Royal Regiment of Fusiliers, between 1982 and 1984. To me he epitomised everything that a true warrior was about. Without wishing to sound cheesy, there's a moment in *Rocky IV* when Adrian, Rocky's wife, turns to him and proclaims that he can't win, that he's up against insurmountable odds. Doubting himself, as all sportsmen do before any true challenge, Rocky responds in a subdued but perfect manner: 'Maybe I can't . . . but in order that he beats me, he's going to have to be prepared to die himself . . . and I'm not sure he's ready to do that.' Nigel Benn fought Gerald McClellan in 1995, at the time the best pound-for-pound fighter in the world. Benn was knocked down twice in the first round. What ensued was one of the most courageous responses the world of sport has ever seen. Going back to his corner, as he steadied himself, and facing a fighter who was leagues ahead of him in ability, Benn knew this was his life's defining moment. Standing silent, looking deep down into the very core of his being, facing fear head-on, he had a choice: to come out prepared to die or capitulate, take the money and be remembered as just another boxer. It was sport at its cruellest and most basic; the moment when your character is on show and being tested to the utmost, and, for all the PR, hype and media angles, there is simply no faking it. Benn's extraordinary courage that night was surpassed only by an example of the phrase I have used above: sport at its cruellest. At the end of the fight, McClellan collapsed with, it was later discovered, a blood clot on the brain. He has never fully recovered.

All the grunting from the garage, my adherence to Rocky-style training montages and cranking out loud music was perhaps a sacrifice my parents were happy to make to get me out of the house. Soon I'd saved up enough to buy myself an elastic resistance work bench (being worried about the misconception that all weights stunt your growth) and mixed my time between bedroom beastings and garage fight club to the accompaniment of soft rock classics from the eighties – belting! But how was I to train? I look at some of the academy lads and apprentice rugby players at Wasps now and I am quite envious that they are given so much accurate information, meaning that no time or unnecessary effort is wasted and that they can reach their physical peak much earlier. Back then it was five-mile runs and circuits, things, it is now known, that couldn't be more detrimental to developing speed and power. At the time I hugely admired Jonathan Davies who had made a successful transition to rugby league. He also played fly half, was physically quite small and yet had a deft turn of speed. I wrote to him and the 'fitness coach' of Widnes at the time to ask what training programmes they followed, just trying to get some advice. Unfortunately I didn't get a reply and so just cracked on with what I thought 'felt' good, learning through trial and error. It wasn't till I got to university and studied physiology that I began to get some decent advice. (Because of my own experiences, I always try to respond to every letter from aspiring youngsters, to help out in any way I can, as without such advice I know how frustrating it can be.)

The whole process I went through in that period made for an enormous amount of wasted effort in terms of its effect on my rugby, but it was a good lesson in mental discipline, if nothing else, and did throw up the odd amusing incident. For all their apparent vision, Watford Council failed to respond to any of my letters requesting some sort of discount for using local sports facilities. Based on earnings from a paper round, or a summer job working in a Watford market bakery, forking out £4 per gym or pool session or £6 to use the local track just wasn't affordable, so I pleaded that as a representative (county) level sportsman who was trying to improve his ability I should be considered for some form of discount. Not getting a reply, not being able to afford the facilities and living about eight miles from them anyway didn't stop me, though. It makes me laugh now to think how Edward and I used to climb the fence and use the track in the pitch dark; and how, if you timed it right, you could follow someone through the turnstiles at Watford Baths before school without paying. I didn't feel guilty then, and I don't feel guilty about it now.

It always amuses and amazes me when I am on tour in countries, such as the United States and especially Australia, to see just how well they cater for sport, identifying it, correctly, as a vital part of national morale and aware of its beneficial effects in other areas, too. In this country, on the other hand, we have underfunded sport for generations; we still seem to view it as more of a hobby or pleasant pastime. Swimmers, for example, need to get up at sparrow's fart to train in the pool, since priority seems to be given instead to menopausal chit-chatters. Unsurprisingly I feel fairly strongly about this and, as well as being an ambassador for the charity Access Sport, I have also joined forces with ELBA (East London Business Alliance) to initiate some sport for primary-age kids in Tower Hamlets.

Once I'd started A levels, there didn't seem to be enough hours in the day. As one who enormously enjoyed the interaction and focus of school, as a teenager with friends away the long summer holidays bored me. I had my share of getting drunk and getting into harmless trouble but I always felt slightly unfulfilled unless I was making the most of my time. I loved learning new things, especially about the countryside; I enjoyed fishing and shooting and would read anything I could get my hands on to further my knowledge.

Apart from biology and anything to do with the human body no other subjects really held my interest, but as I'd learned to discipline myself I worked hard, enjoying the satisfaction of doing well at something I wasn't that good at or had to push myself in order to do. At the time, you had to keep one eye on university but the choice of career afterwards was far from clear. Rugby had not yet gone professional and was still technically an amateur sport. Top English players tended to 'work' for main club sponsors but I knew fairly early on that I wouldn't be content in the traditional nine-to-five rat race. When the school arranged for me to meet a representative of the army board, fairly quickly I was off to RCB (Regular Commissions Board) to see if I had what it took to be offered a place at Sandhurst.

That was one of my first trips away from home by myself and, despite it only being for a few days, I found it enthralling, challenging and enjoyable. Previously the army had held absolutely no interest for me. I'd grown up in a period when, apart from the Falklands, being in the Army meant lots of training, theoretical warfare and deterrents, but no real action. It seemed, for the time being at least, that the army with the biggest and the most toys won. Additionally, having a grandfather (Dad's dad had been in the forces) who was more Albert Steptoe than ruddy-faced colonel meant that my enduring image of army camps tended to be one of tired, desolate warehouses rather than the excitement of life under fire and the reward of personal ambition attained. I attended a three-day course in which every aspect of my ability and character was assessed. There was of course the obligatory basic fitness test, and command tasks which examined individuals' leadership or management skills. However, what I was surprised to find, and thus most intrigued by, were the mathematical, general knowledge, current affairs and problem-solving activities, which culminated with interviews and cross-examination from a board of senior army bods. Obviously they were trying to assess and report on your all-round character and ability.

After a proper old-style dinner in the officers' mess, we were sent back to await our results. It turned out that I'd scored well enough to be offered a bursary through university and the guarantee of a minimum short-service commission. In practical terms that meant a £1,500-a-year tax-free loan with no interest or redemption penalties. Thus with this new-found 'wealth' I was proud to be able to detach myself from my parents' financial teat.

Interestingly enough, as grades at GCSE and A levels become increasingly higher year on year, with top students all seeming to get multiple A stars, it is becoming harder for universities to decide who to offer places to. Thus, as some top schools are now looking for more than just these two 'educational milestones', an increasing number of savvy, ambitious youngsters are using their RCB reports to help them get into university.

I loved my last few years at school, and after A levels, in the summer of 1995, we went off to Canada on a rugby tour. We were an exceptionally tight-knit group of friends and what better way to end seven brilliant years together.

Although things have changed now in what is the sterile, highly managed world of professional rugby, touring for the amateur or junior has always been the most enjoyable part of the game, what with the shenanigans youngsters get up to on away trips, with plenty of parties, booze and that particular ingredient notably absent from an all-boys school: girls! However, it was being billeted with your opposite number that ultimately threw up the most memorable moments. Flying into the beautiful city of Calgary was sophisticated enough, but during the trip east to Toronto we stumbled on the odd interesting character.

As captain of the team in Calgary I had to stay at the opposing chairman's house; although he had no kids, this was mitigated by the fact that he had an original AC Cobra 427 and he was happy to drive me around in it and drop me off at the others' parties.

Everyone wanted their billet to have older sisters. Further into the trip, in the flat prairies of the Saskatchewan and Alberta border we came to a redneck town called Lloydminster. I loved the ruggedness of the place and the people were brilliant. I remember the club's liaison officer there was called Dwaine, as was his son and probably the rest of the family too, but at that stage it was too embarrassing to ask. Naturally, because they looked like they'd auditioned for the film *Deliverance*, and because they were also keen hunters, we paired their son with the only vegetarian in the team.

My younger brother Edward played scrum half on the trip, and being the cute younger one, and so laid-back that he was almost horizontal, the local girls were rather fond of him. Although at the time he looked more like Beavis or Butthead, he took well to the Alberta steaks and cold beer, coming back a good stone heavier than he left.

Another lad was billeted with hardy foresters, who had their own lake and speedboat. He was the shy type and, although forced to water-ski in freezing conditions, thought it would be rude to tell them he couldn't swim.

It's said the sense of smell is the one most closely linked to memory; if so, that would explain why one incident, which can be described literally as toilet humour, sticks in mine. As mentioned, we landed in Calgary and drove east across the increasing heat of the Canadian prairie, stopping at various spots on the way. After an especially heavy night of steak and beer one of the lads failed to notice the Out of Service sign the driver had posted next to the coach toilet. Consequently, as the lad's remnants sat on the heating sheet of metal, for the entire six-hour trip we were subjected to the intense aroma of baked poo!

It was, quite simply, a brilliant few weeks, in which the true nature of touring and sampling the local culture were embraced. It still pains people now when I put a bit of Garth Brooks or Johnny

Cash on in the car when giving them a lift. The tour was a fitting and successful way to say goodbye to one stage in my life and to look forward to the next. For most of us that meant leaving home and university; for me that meant Bristol.

Chapter 3

Bristol – and England

A s with so many children when they leave the nest, it was with some trepidation – but mostly excitement – that I travelled down the M4 to Bristol. It was now autumn 1995; my older brother, Tom, had already been there a year so I was reasonably familiar with where everything was and how to find my way to the sports field, though I knew absolutely no one else and so set about making pals.

I spent my first year at Churchill Hall, renowned for its social scene, but in a slightly less attractive setting than the cloistered sandstone of neighbouring Wills Hall. I spent most of my time between the two (Wills had better food), and I can't write about this period without smiling and remembering how happy a time it was. As most students will verify, during one's first year the academic side of things is really only a slight inconvenience for the other stuff – getting drunk, making mates, meeting girls and playing sport. The first evening we were addressed by the Hall's warden (he would later give me a slightly more personal audience when after a night of heavy drinking a few of us broke into the kitchens to find something to eat). Afterwards, most people stepped boldly into the bar to meet their new mates.

'Errm . . .' slightly awkwardly, never particularly adept at idle chit-chat or small talk, particularly without the help of alcohol, '. . . right then . . . sod it. Really sorry to disturb you, but you look reasonably normal. Fancy a drink?' Seven pints of Old Peculiar later and I was best friends with Sebastian Lauzier from Gloucestershire, a keen rugby man, and, along with a number of others, one of a genuinely lovely bunch with whom I remain good friends.

On arrival at Bristol it soon became clear what calibre of student the university attracted. When I was picked to play in my first university game, my name was posted as Josh Rhys-Lewsey (Rhys being my elder brother's middle name). It turned out that it was assumed everyone had a double-barrelled name unless otherwise stated. The reputation the university had for rugby was also fierce, with Kyran Bracken having recently been capped by England after graduating. The back line of the team at the time – Alex King, Mark Denney, Fraser Waters and myself – would be the mainstay of the Bristol and then the Wasps line-up for some years afterwards.

On the first day of training, Bob Reeves, the director of sport, asked all the freshers to stand on the line.

'Everyone who's played county level representative rugby, step forward.'

Everyone stepped forward.

'Everyone who's played divisional level, step forward.'

About ten people stepped forward.

'Everyone who has played full international representative schoolboy rugby, step forward.'

Only one stepped forward.

Huh? I'd been at that final trial a few months earlier and to be honest I didn't recognise him – hardly surprising when you think about it since the bloke who stepped forward was clearly lying – but I enjoyed repeating the story when I was best man at his wedding eleven years later. That was my first introduction to a certain David Barry Johnson (DJ), who it also transpired was on my course. Loud, brash, rude and cocky, I took an instant dislike to him, but in the end it was impossible not to laugh with – and at – this unique character, and we enjoyed many memorable incidents together thereafter.

During my first year at university I was travelling back home to Hertfordshire at the weekends and playing representative Colts (Under 19) rugby for the county. Hertfordshire had always been very much a minnow in the county game and consequently, with a very good side in our age group that had a realistic chance of winning silverware, we all learned very quickly that the selectors would do all they could to get us back home to play. This meant that we could be creative with our travelling expenses. Joe Worsley, who I'd played with and against since we were six, lived with his mother in Welwyn. Playing and training with Wasps, he had decided to forgo university for the opportunity of playing professional rugby immediately. Somehow, however, he managed to convince the powers that be that he had an elderly gran in Scotland who he cared for on a weekly basis. My future flatmate Andy Dailly played flanker and, coming from the impressive Haileybury School, inherited the standard vehicle of choice for any self-respecting student – an old maroon 1.2 VW Golf. Andy was housed at Wills and soon we also discovered that a mate of ours, Humfrey Hunter, was also qualified by birth to play for Herts. As a result we fabricated some of the best fictional journeys heard since Tolkien and shared Andy's car to and from games, even turning the ignition off on the downhill bits to save fuel!

The gents at Herts did, of course, know what we were up to, but a final at Twickenham was fair exchange (even if we were beaten by East Midlands), and it at least meant we ate more between games than just ketchup sandwiches. In terms of my physical stature, I was now starting to fill out. All the early training had got me to a certain level but that only really began to pay off when I got to university and first started doing proper weight training.

Coming from an all-boys school and a male-dominated household, I have to admit that I found girls alluring, confusing – and, of course, terrifying. Every year I meet up with my mates from school for the coveted 'Chief Challenge', usually involving a game of golf followed by beers in the Fox and Hounds at Croxley Green and a curry at the Standard Tandoori. If you substitute the golf for a team sport then effectively it is identical to the way we spent most Saturdays when we were at school. If you then factor in a week in class and Sundays playing rugby too, then, aside from Mum, you suddenly realise that you went weeks without even talking to a woman. So, you can imagine what I was like on arriving at university; picture a more bumbling Hugh Grant in *Four Weddings and a Funeral* sort of figure and you'll have an idea of the embarrassment and unease I exuded at the time, especially around any girls I liked or thought pretty.

'Hi, Josh, how're things?'

'Errrmmmmm . . . errr . . . fine thanks . . .' (Proceeding to neck the drink that was in my hand. Awkward silence.) 'Fancy a drink?' (Something to say.)

'Yes, please, Josh, that's very kind.'

'So, then . . . errm . . . errr . . . studies going well?' (Oh, my God, did I really say that? You sad bastard.)

'Well, it's been a bit manic and with the Freshers Ball and all . . .'

(Say something, quick.) 'What did you go as?' (It was black tie, you imbecile! That's it, panic.) 'Here we go, that's yours . . .' (Proceeding to neck my drink again as it saved me having to talk, or hoping that it might give just a little Dutch courage.) 'Ooh errrrr, is that the . . . got to . . . err . . . lovely to see you again – Bye.' (Rushing off to hide and self-loathe.)

Thinking about it makes me laugh now, but in the same cringe-making way as watching an excruciating episode of Ricky Gervais' *The Office*. I haven't really touched on personal relationships so far, but when you consider that my first date was when I was fourteen – Dad dropped me off at the cinema and, seeing my anxiety, suggested, 'Treat her like you would your sister, son' (worthy advice, except of course I didn't have a sister and therefore had absolutely no idea what this meant), – university was a case of in at the deep end with no waterwings.

As far as rugby was concerned, the game had recently gone professional, and the 1995 World Cup, hosted by South Africa, had exploded with this new word on everyone's lips. In the shape of dynamic athletes with phenomenal skills and ability New Zealand and South Africa demonstrated what professionalism meant and where the game was going at last. Despite them not winning the tournament, I remember watching the All Blacks in the semi-final against England and feeling enormously excited about the future of the game, and confident that I could have a role in it. Out went the phrase 'percentage rugby' and in came new keywords: ambition, skill, speed and power. For the All Blacks, Jonah Lomu and Zinzan Brooke, the latter with his ability to score from long drop goals, epitomised these qualities, and the whole team's level of skill and athleticism was way ahead of any other.

In England, some rugby clubs took the lessons on board more quickly than others. Now, for the first time, rugby offered a chance of making a living, but, despite being offered a professional role to stay at Wasps (I'd played for them since the age of eighteen), I decided I didn't want to spend all my time travelling up and down from university and thus opted to knock on the door of the local club, Bristol. The conversation I had with them effectively boiled down to: 'Fine, let's have a look at you in the second team for a couple of games first, though.' So my first proper professional game was for Bristol United against my freshers mates in the university second team at Coombe Dingle Sports Complex. To the day I die I will never forget Phil Adams' speech before the game; just bear in mind that, as arguably the heartbeat of the club and a top bloke to his core, the grizzly old warhorse was as broad a Bristolian as they come and a hard-toiling plasterer by day . . .

'I f**king *hate* stuuuudents! Look, these lot think it's funny to put traffic cones on statues, run over your car setting off the alarm, pay for chips with a cheque, pay no tax on their beer, sit in bed all day and then at Christmas have the goddamn gurt'en audacity to come round your 'ouse asking for money f**king carol singing!'

The game that ensued was – and there is no other way to describe it – the most brutal and amusing assault on students I had ever witnessed. Funnily enough, by the time the ball reached me at full back, there weren't many students left on their feet to stop us walking in tries.

For the next year or so it was student rugby on Wednesday afternoons, fitting in club training where possible and playing in what was then the First Division for Bristol RFC on Saturdays. Halcyon days for a young man, during which I managed to mix the best of being a carefree student with earning money from doing something I loved. On paper, Bristol had a phenomenal team, but the remit of being professional hadn't really sunk in to a talented bunch of lads who were, frankly, too busy enjoying themselves to make the most of their potential. Sometimes I used to walk on to the pitch literally crying with laughter. There were some brilliant characters in the team, the polar opposite of those you encountered in the sheltered existence of student life in leafy Clifton.

Most stories around that time involved in some way the effervescent Mark 'Ronnie' Regan. People say that whenever he's around morale will always be high. Imagine, then, the place with ten or twelve Ronnies.

For five minutes at the beginning of every training session, as soon as the coach walked on to get things going the senior jokers would take the group off to another corner of the field for the process to start all over again. Bearing in mind this lot included thirty-five-year-old men it was so childish I'd giggle incessantly.

One pre-season, we were training at Coombe Dingle when the freshers trials were taking place. The first-year lacrosse team jogged past on their warm-up.

'Oooooohhhhhhhhh . . . Get your rat out!' The girls from Roedean, Malvern and Benenden etc. rapidly changed direction as the rest of us rolled around in hysterics.

Kevin Maggs, a hard-running and straight-talking local lad, was a kerb layer by day and had a reputation around the bars and clubs of Broadmead as being fairly tasty in a scrap. One day a bouncer from one of the local nightclubs joined us for training, having had, with some of his colleagues, an 'incident' with Maggsy during the off season. Needless to say he didn't come back after that session.

Ronnie and Sharpy (Alan Sharp) were best of mates, but always at each other. Once or twice they actually, genuinely, fell out when their constant banter crossed the line into something more personal. It was like two little kids being pulled apart in the playground. It was all 'You started it.' 'No, *you* started it.' 'You said som'ing against my ma.' 'You said som'ing about *my* Mir [Ronnie's wife].' And then, as soon as it had started, 'Aaaahhhhhh! Bab. Had youse!' (Back into play mode again.) 'Ooohhh, I got you first, "Kidney"' – and everything was back to normal.

Bristol was such a cracking place, but the upper echelons of the club were inefficient and the loss of the Memorial Ground to Bristol Rovers Football Club for just £10,000 left a bitter taste in the mouths of those who had Bristol's best interests at heart.

Ultimately it was perhaps this lack of ambition at the club that led me back to Wasps and made others leave in the pursuit of silverware. In the future, Bristol would once again be a force to be reckoned with, becoming one of the giants of the English game, but at the time that was far off.

Robert Jones, a childhood hero of mine and the catalyst of the legendary Lions brawl of '89 in the second test against Australia (for more on this see 'My Greatest XV') had recently signed for Bristol and was fairly quickly made captain. The first game of the season I was naturally nervous and found myself in the huddle with the old stalwarts, our hearts thumping. Rob calmly took the mascot (a seventeen-year-old girl, taller than him) to the centre spot, waving and smiling sweetly for the cameras. On returning to the circle and detecting our anxiety, he dispelled it, joking, 'Don't worry, lads, I got her number!'

Although I had always played number 10 in my youth, with the need to get the best players on the park – Alex King being established at fly half at the university and me being pretty nippy – I was moved to full back. Although missing the decision-making opportunities, I enjoyed the extra running freedom it gave me, compared to the tight confines of the midfield.

Paul Hull had been the full back for Bristol and had been a revelation on the recent (1994) England tour to South Africa before injury cruelly robbed him of what would surely have been many more international honours and accolades. He was also enormously supportive, helpful and, on reflection, wise with regard to the way he handled me. Incoming was this rather cocky non-local lad who threatened his position and thought he knew best. Although initially somewhat guarded, Paul was always on hand to lend advice, give his time for extra work on my weaker areas and pass on invaluable technical hints on elements of the full-back's game that only experience can teach. He also had a fatherly chat to me when we bumped into each other at Sainsbury's one afternoon. His advice was offered entirely without concern for his own ego or thoughts of self-preservation; it was about choosing a position and sticking to it – something that would resonate clearly throughout my career as it progressed.

It is no small coincidence that Bristol, now back in the Premiership, always difficult to beat and built on the cornerstone of England's biggest rugby city, has one of the most successful defences, orchestrated by this bright and unassuming man who I'm sure will at some stage become a successful international coach.

The club was, though, representative of Bristol. People rightly played for the city and its community and the very fact of being a Bristolian brought identity to what had become the sleeping giant of the English game. The squad was formed predominantly of local lads, supplemented by a sprinkling of talented students, the odd import or 'emmets' (settlers not from the west!). It was this sense of community that I most enjoyed representing. Bath and Glouces-ter, as the heartbeat of their respective cities, have it in abundance; Leicester and Northampton too, to some extent, but it is this element that, in playing for the nomadic Wasps, I have missed most. Wasps is a special club, with loyal support, but it tends to be made up of the unique characters who've been involved with the shirt and an eclectic mix of fans from all over the country rather than the representation of one geographical area. Whether by coincidence or otherwise, while the club was named after an animal as was fashionable at the time, the name also fitted nicely with the geographical districts that surrounded its base in north-west London – Wembley, Alperton, Sudbury and Perivale. As an inevitable consequence of being a London-based club, it has however drifted away from its original foundations to find fans and support. Warren Gatland once described Wasps as a foster home for waifs, strays and social misfits, which in hindsight probably explains why they signed me.

* * *

As I mentioned earlier, I played for the university on most Wednesday afternoons and would then shoot over to the Memorial Ground for the evening training sessions. The thought of evening training is probably something alien to the full-time pros of the modern game, but as some regular players were still combining their daytime trade with this new idea of pay to play, it made sense to do a few sessions under lights when all could attend. Firsts versus seconds is always a recipe for disaster, but with the extra incentive of £500 pay to play on the following Saturday at stake, you can understand why it was more akin to rollerball than professional sport. 'Look, lads, I know they're your mates, but if you kick your number in the head, they're out for Saturday, and it's a monkey in your sky rocket!'

Ed Morrison, the charismatic and popular Bristol referee, would come down and do his best to adjudicate for forty minutes, often cutting the session short if it deteriorated into serious conflict. Ed is a cracking rugby man, still has a big influence on the modern game and was once caught saying at a Sevens tournament, with Bristol's opposition knocking the ball on, 'Scrum down, OUR ball.'

For me it was all simply great fun. During the week I was a student living the life and training when I could, but at weekends and in the holidays I was a paid sportsman, representing the city. But it was not all party and play. By this stage I had decided that I wanted to be as good as I could possibly be, and again trained exceptionally hard, often sacrificing the 'big event' opportunities in order to become better on the field. I don't regret such missed opportunities and I am certainly not jealous of today's students who make the most of theirs at university. Despite having to work very hard to manage my time between rugby and study, I'd like to think that I got a good balance between achievement and enjoyment. Although it isn't entirely impossible to balance the two today, even if you are willing to work hard enough – and sometimes people aren't – there is no doubt that it's a more difficult thing to do now as the demands and the time required to achieve higher standards are much greater. I was to learn just how difficult it could be a little later, when I was trying to do justice to both the army and to rugby. Often in life you have to make choices and sacrifices. There are lots of things we'd like to do and we probably make a reasonable go of them, rushing to do everything at once. But to be as good as you can be at one thing more often than not means sacrificing others. However, at this early stage in the professional game studying for a proper university degree was just about possible as long as your employer was flexible.

My second year at university was spent in the flat my brother had vacated in glorious Royal York Crescent. Now playing regularly for the first team and being on an unspendable £10,000 a year, I treated myself to a new car on a club lease deal. A purple convertible Rover 1.6se was, on reflection, an ugly car and a terrible choice, but it had its benefits. It was a vaguely adult-looking car and that meant that, with some bribable Bristol rugby fans on security at the professors' university walk, DJ and I could drive to lectures and pass it off as the Vice-Chancellor's in his often empty car parking spot!

That season, 1996–7, was a frustrating one at the club and the formerly naïve and irresponsible rookie was now witnessing sackings, redundancies and the repercussions of regularly losing in the competitive First Division. Bristol, potentially England's largest rugby club, was in a relegation play-off against Bedford.

We won both home and away, but what impressed us all was how much diligence, effort and professionalism had gone into the week in terms of the preparation, training and recovery. Martin Corry was club captain at the time and rightly questioned why such an attitude couldn't be applied to every game. The home game was incredibly intense; at least it felt so at the time. I received a yellow card from Steve Lander, the referee. I was enraged at the injustice and though back then it meant no more than a warning, and certainly not the ten minutes in the sin bin it does now, I still felt it unjustified. This is what happened: Mike Rayer, the former Welsh international full back, was lying next to me in a ruck and someone obviously did something to him to which he took exception. It certainly wasn't me and though he came at me swinging punches, I was conscious in such a tense game of the importance of not giving away penalties or, worse, being sent off, so I kept my temper and didn't throw a single punch (though in hindsight, as I was disciplined by the association anyway, I wish that I had). The range of feelings I experienced that day was exhausting and for an emotional young man who'd been made so welcome by this passionate rugby community the sense of relief, responsibility, pride and happiness at avoiding the drop was overwhelming.

There had been weekly meetings throughout the season involving both players and staff on what was going wrong and how to put it right. Those meetings obviously didn't produce the answer: by the end of the following season, when I was away on tour and doing my finals, the club finally succumbed to the inevitable and dropped from the top flight for the first time in its illustrious history.

However, to add to the euphoria of survival in '97 I was also selected to play for England 'A' against Ireland and Scotland in the 'A' team Five Nations – being considered a fly half by the representative powers. The Under 21 tour of Australia also beckoned, managed by a certain C. Woodward. More on him later in the book, but my first impressions of Clive were of a professional, challenging and far-seeing coach who encouraged us to do the unexpected – 'take the shackles off' and 'give it a lash'. It was music to my ears. We lost two of our key front-five players in the opening few minutes of the test match against Australia, and along with them the test match, but it was an enjoyable learning experience and a fascinating introduction to a unique individual who was eventually to have a huge influence on my life. I really admired Clive and was delighted to be called up.

One year on and Clive was doing the main job. He had co-coached the Under 21 team with the unsung Rob Smith of Wasps in 1996. Rob is one of the all-too-often unmentioned reasons for Wasps' continual production of top-level English talent. In my opinion his measured and pragmatic balance complemented Clive's vision on that tour and I thought he'd be in with a shout of playing Clive's sidekick at the next level.

I was finishing off my studies in 1998, ready for the next step and going through the rigmarole of trying to fit finals around international selection. I asked to see the faculty head.

'Hello, sir, I'm here to discuss the matter of doing my finals. The thing is I've been picked to go on the senior international tour of the southern hemisphere. As such, would it be possible to do the exams either before I went, or perhaps when I got back?'

Being a university that prided itself on its academic reputation, Bristol was under no circumstances willing to compromise its standards.

'Your choice, Mr Lewsey, is either to do the exams as the others would, logistics permitting, or wait until next year. If this itinerary is correct you will just have landed when the others sit their exams; as such you will be invigilated by your tour manager and sit them under his jurisdiction as close as physically possible to the time that we administer them here.'

So having just landed, jet-lagged and with the imposing presence of Roger Uttley snoring loudly in the corner, I sat my physiology finals. I couldn't help wondering as I did so if I could not have somehow brokered a better deal.

Clive had, in fact, selected me to be on the bench for the first match. My head, it must be said, was all over the place that week and it certainly wasn't the ideal preparation for my first ever international. It showed in training, too; when trying to remember the physiology of the renal system, the chemical composition of atrioventricular transmitters and so on, my mind went completely blank and I couldn't remember any of the backs' moves. As such, though I was obviously disappointed, Clive pulled me and put Alex King in instead. It was the right decision, but I can't help wondering if I could have stayed at home for that week in the first place, done my exams properly like everyone else, and joined the touring squad the following week.

It was a blessing in disguise as it turned out. The record 76–0 defeat to Australia was the start, and indeed end, of many players' international careers.

I was picked to play the following week against New Zealand. Jonny Wilkinson was at 10 and I played 12 outside him. I'd never played 12 in my life, but who better to start against than New Zealand on their home patch?

Life had very much been a case of sink or swim up to this point and rugby was clearly going the same way. Compared with the Kiwis, we were vastly inferior physically, and tactically the game we played week in week out was from a different era to the one these glitzy athletes played in. Teams in the southern hemisphere had for a long period been professional in all but name. Underpowered and without our first-choice team because of injury, it is not surprising we were unsuccessful. I do however look back at that tour as a real test of the temperament of those who at least had the self-belief, competitiveness and mental strength to play at that level.

People talk of an under-strength unit, but when you factor in names such as Vickery, Rowntree, Greening, Cockerill, Archer, Grewcock, Clarke, Sanderson, Ojomoh, Dawson, Wilkinson, Perry, Healey and Stimpson, you realise that it wasn't without ability. The fact of the matter is that at the time all three of the southern hemisphere sides – Australia, New Zealand and South Africa – were considerably better than England, and would have been even if the full-strength first team had toured. The biggest difference was in the physical conditioning. Clive highlighted this fairly early on and, give credit where it is due, by the time we lifted the World Cup five years later, England, under the scrutiny of Dave Reddin, were the best-conditioned team in the competition.

Clive had always been quite impressed by my approach to conditioning and, at my first-ever senior England session, in which I was of course eager to please, he made a special request of me.

'Right then, lads, gather round. We need to be the fittest team in the world, carrying no excess weight. Josh, take your top off.'

'Errrrr, what?'

'Take your top off!'

'Errrr, you're joking, right?'

'No, I'm deadly serious. TAKE YOUR TOP OFF!'

Mortified, pleading with him silently not to make me do this, aware that it's my first session and I'm trying to make friends, I shut my eyes, followed orders, and waited for the players' backlash.

'Now, that is the body I want to see on everyone playing for this team.'

Player's voice: 'Josh, you're still a c**t.' (As if I didn't know!)

My first cap was at Carisbrook, Dunedin, in a stadium full of students, and the atmosphere was brilliant. Unfortunately, the whole day seemed to pass so quickly that I can hardly remember it. I do recall feeling enormously emotional during the national anthems. I feel it to this day and to my mind the moment someone stops getting a tingle down their spine when they sing their national anthem before a game it's time to give up wearing the jersey. However, having built myself up to this heightened state, I was, on reflection, too geed up, as I then spent the first third of the game feeling slightly nervous and inhibited. We lost that game 64–22. I took that lesson into the following week. They say there is no substitute for experience, and in my opinion this is especially true in terms of mental preparation and the understanding of the mindset that suits particular occasions. There is a fine balance between being 'up for the task' – blood racing, ready to explode physically – and staying measured, analytical, able to make the correct decisions at the right time, under pressure. That's not to say that with all the experience in the world you don't make mistakes or are in the wrong state of mind, but when things go badly, with experience you tend to think more and have a better perspective and better coping mechanisms the older you get.

The following week was the final game of a certain Sean Fitzpatrick before he retired, at the home of NZ rugby – Eden Park, Auckland. I played 10 as Jonny had got himself injured. This was the game on the tour that I took most pride in. I'd learned the lesson from the previous week and realised that international rugby is, put simply, about 'fronting up': mentally daring to play at your limit, not within your shell. I genuinely felt that, despite the end result, I could walk off the park with my head held high.

We started well and, though generally considered to be outgunned, we had a disallowed try on the stroke of half-time that would've put us in the lead going into the break. Inevitably, in the last quarter NZ ran away with it, their superior fitness showing as they capitalised on our mistakes and went on to win 40–10. But a few hours after the game, drunk in a bar somewhere in Auckland, I remember that feeling of quiet contentment and satisfaction you get when you know you've done OK.

I haven't watched the game since and, to be honest, I probably made a few mistakes and didn't actually play all that well. But at the time I knew that, regardless of all other things, I at least had the heart to play and even excel at the higher level, with the self-belief that, regardless of our poor results and criticism back at home, I'd discovered something very positive about myself. Jonah Lomu was not the same beast as he had been in 1995, when he so famously brushed England and Tony Underwood aside in a World Cup match, but he was still the symbol of New Zealand superiority and, with twenty minutes left, had broken clear. I was corner-flagging and was the last line of cover defence. He had two unmarked players outside him but thought, quite understandably, that at full tilt and at over nineteen stone he'd bulldoze this blond waif in front of him. Like I said, to me international rugby was about fronting up and so I threw myself as hard as I could into his path. Fortunately he hit the ground and in doing so spilled the ball forward. The reality was that, like everyone who goes through good times and bad, his form wasn't what it had been three years earlier and all I'd done was not miss a tackle, but as it was him and something so visual, it was played over and over again by the New Zealand media as 'the moment Lomu lost his aura of invincibility'. Ruthless as the Kiwis are, with a myriad of talent to call on, subsequently he was dropped.

I can't honestly remember what hotel we stayed in, but on stumbling back there on my lonesome, in the early hours, a busload of Maori boys stopped next to me on a dark street. Realising that most of them looked like extras from the film *Once Were Warriors*, and stinking of booze, I feared that in my posh suit and tanned brogues I was in for a kicking.

'Ah, bro, get in, man!'

'You're that Pom, aren't you?'

Still on the pavement, uncertain whether this was a kind offer, or an aggressive order, I said, 'Listen, pal, I've already taken a kicking once today, so if you're going to give me one, can you at least drop me back at my hotel?'

'No, man, join us. You're awesome, man.'

I presumed they thought I was someone else, but refusing the kind hospitality of twenty-odd huge drunken 'bros' was probably not the wisest decision for someone in my current predicament.

After taking a customary sip from what could have been straight meths, one of my new best mates shoved the first copy of the morning paper into my hand. On the front cover was a photograph that my parents later bought and framed for my twenty-first and under it was the caption 'Last Man Standing'. The picture was of me with my back to the camera, facing nine All Blacks coming at me with the ball. It may seem a little self-engrossed to mention only myself at such a time, particularly when we lost all our games and, inevitably, I made my fair share of mistakes both on and off the field, but it was a time I look back on with pride. At that moment, those strangers on the other side of the world recognised and respected me for something I'd done. I was someone.

The next week we played South Africa on a wet and muddy Newlands in Cape Town. The theme was very much damage limitation, hence our dull tactics. We lost 18–10 in an incredibly boring affair, during which, after my self-belief of the previous week, I was left deflated after having a kick charged down by Joost van der Westhuizen. By this stage, however, considering what had gone on before, the score-line was at least not a complete embarrassment and everyone just wanted to get on the plane, having been away for over six weeks.

As with all good tours back in those days, we had a mock-court session in which Richard Cockerill, Gareth Archer and Phil Greening were judge, bailiff and executioner. Being a somewhat cocksure youngster I was of course accused of various crimes against being a good bloke etc. Unsurprisingly found guilty as charged, I was given the choice of 'William Hague, or the bald turkey'. With my graduation only two days away, the various garden parties and my parents attending, I obviously chose the 'bald turkey'. 'Tough. William Hague it is!'

'Please don't, I genuinely couldn't care less, but my mother would be mortified!'

For all the words of praise from Clive Woodward about my physique at the start of the tour, I sure as hell wasn't strong enough when I needed to be! Archer, Grewcock, Rowntree, Darren Crompton and others pinned me down while Richard Cockerill did his best, or indeed worst, impression of Nicky Clarke with the shears.

There are therefore no graduation photographs of me at my parents' house, as, fresh from the tour, and with the cuts and scars to prove it, I looked halfway between a Devil's Island convict and a cage fighter. DJ and the others took great delight in my embarrassment as we stood by the Wills Memorial Building in our Medical Faculty robes in June 1998, a fitting farewell to an amazing and eventful three years in Bristol.

Chapter 4

Wilderness

LEAVING BRISTOL WAS obviously a significant step, but with my friends all graduating to posh jobs in the City, taking that first step on the corporate ladder or just generally gravitating to the Big Smoke, moving back to Wasps felt like the natural thing for me to do. I was now an international rugby player and, though by today's standards not wealthy in the least, I had enough money in my pocket to buy my first property. I felt enormously grown-up, but as far as youthful exuberance went, I'd always been a bit boring, and so within a few weeks was the proud owner of a two-bedroom flat in a Victorian mansion block in Chiswick. It was a good stock property, albeit somewhat geographically removed from the frantic nightlife and the debauchery enjoyed by my friends in Fulham. In hindsight, maybe as a young man in London for the first time I should have found a place closer to the vibe and energy of London's West End. But that isn't exactly conducive to the life of a professional athlete with money in his pocket, and being an obsessive, driven character it might have been too easy to lose a sense of reality. So it's probably just as well that I ended up where I did.

At the time training took place at Wasps' original ground of Sudbury. It was then, as now, far from the salubrious surroundings one expected of a top European club, no more than a collection of Portakabins, tired facilities and a place for local dogs to crap! Game day was however somewhat different. Under the new ownership of Chris Wright, we were now part of the same stable as Queens Park Rangers, who were in the sixties and seventies, with Rodney Marsh and the like in their team, the epitome of west London cool. Wasps sharing their ground, Loftus Road, was typical of the new trend for rugby clubs, adopting the fast and 'flat' playing surfaces that were less field-like than traditional rugby pitches. Based in Shepherd's Bush, Loftus Road never had the leafy, family feel of a rugby ground, but being reasonably central it was great for your social life straight after a game. If you were fortunate to find your car still parked outside the ground after leaving it there for a few hours, you would head for the delights of SW6; you can do that sort of thing in your early twenties without feeling any the worse for wear the following week.

Nigel Melville, the former Wasps and England scrum half, was director of rugby at the club, an astute man who encouraged us to play an attacking game. Though a young team, we were predominantly English and already had the basic spine – Green, Shaw, Dallaglio, Worsley, Volley, King, Waters and me – that stayed together for more than ten years with eventual unprecedented success.

We were a big club, but in truth most of the players felt somewhat unfulfilled by the recent transition to professionalism. Having balanced a full-time degree course with playing professional rugby, I, for one, had boundless energy that I felt was not being fully utilised. The off-field structuring, accountability and professionalism championed in the international game by Clive Woodward had not yet been introduced to club rugby and as such the players were not satisfied with merely playing PlayStation in their spare time, but looked further afield to fulfil themselves.

Those being selected internationally inevitably had the extra demands on their time with sponsors and appearances, but for those of us merely playing full-time club rugby there seemed to be an awful lot of hours to fill between one game and the next. I was really looking forward to the prospect of being able to concentrate on just one thing and doing that as well as I could. However, as history later showed, we weren't enormously challenged or stimulated. It is human nature in such circumstances for people to be happiest when they are being challenged. Here, players weren't satisfied that they were conditioning physically as well as they might – they weren't being pushed – and were going off to do their own thing, training elsewhere.

We were a good side with some exceptional players, but we weren't playing to our capacity, so, despite lifting two domestic trophies (the Tetley's Bitter Cup) in 1999 and 2000, frankly they weren't the League or European titles that players of our calibre would have been more satisfied with. It is this collective ambition and determination to succeed that ultimately changed Wasps into the most successful English club side in history.

I have found that this ambition and determination to succeed can be misunderstood by coaches and other players; they often take a natural dislike to individuals who display such qualities, seeing them as difficult or challenging and certainly not easy to get on with. Historically, players who have been prepared to speak their minds openly (rather than behind people's backs) in order to see improvements made have been marginalised, highlighting management's weakness: the failure to control and harness creative players and to enhance their skills. The danger when that happens is that you're left with a bunch of amiable personalities unwilling to challenge each other and prepared to accept what the coach says without question, so once the pressure is on in a big match, for example, you're found wanting in terms of leadership, strategy and, most importantly, success.

That is why I salute those coaches who have managed to harness such talents, getting the balance right by encouraging dynamic player ownership while retaining respect and control. I'll touch more on the dynamics of such leadership later in the book; meanwhile, however, the word coming out of the England camp at the time was that, thanks to my personality, my face didn't fit! Why? Maybe I challenged them too much. I genuinely don't know to this day why it was. Apparently, confidential reports had been compiled by the RFU about every individual and, though their contents were never revealed, they seemed at the time to be the making or breaking of players' entire careers. Why not judge people on what they do on the field instead?

A few years later, Warren Gatland came to Wasps and immediately impressed me with his managerial ability: brutal on occasions, cunning and calculating but always, always, fair; he judged you in the light of his own experiences not on mere hearsay. That's all we players want and it is part of the culture we trust and respect the most. If someone stepped out of line, he'd speak bluntly to them, explaining their misdemeanours and demanding they put things right. The reality is that in this environment people seldom step out of line; given trust and responsibility, few then choose to abuse them. Even now when I help coach Richmond women's team I receive reports on players from the RFU. I try my best to take them on board but find myself frustrated at some of the comments about certain players' personalities rather than their technical ability.

What also angered me hugely at the time was that, in my opinion, there were players being selected for England who, quite frankly, weren't performing for their clubs. It seemed a case that if your face fitted and you were winning, unless you did something catastrophic, or, worse still, as a fringe player dared to speak your mind and challenge the status quo, you actually had to work harder to get yourself out of the team than to stay in it. Ultimately, people judge on results, and by now England had really started to remove the shackles, becoming the most dynamic and creative team in the world. They were by no means the finished article, but were regularly blowing away teams in the Five and from 2000 the Six Nations and had begun to beat the southern hemisphere teams more regularly than ever before.

My anger really just stemmed from pure jealousy. England were playing a type of game that I loved and one I was convinced that I was suited to. You could watch and marvel at the sheer confidence and audacity with which the team ran the ball from all corners of the field. It looked enjoyable, the sort of rugby I'd always wanted to play, and was just desperate to be part of. But I wasn't being selected for the senior team.

I tried endlessly to find out what I had to do to get selected, and I'm not ashamed to admit I tried telephoning and writing to Clive Woodward on several occasions, for perfectly legitimate reasons. It is not cool to do such a thing, nor in the professional age is it common practice to break ranks in order to get answers, but in any case they weren't forthcoming. In my defence, it was my career, and the determination to succeed consumed me. I became increasingly resentful and untrusting as some of those playing in a way I thought was consistently average for their clubs continued to be selected for the international side. The Bath connection seemed to be a rubber stamp for the national squad, with Andy Robinson, Brian Ashton and Clive Woodward all having been involved there. Selectors could perhaps justify their choice of players from Bath because they knew players from that club better than players from other clubs. But for players from other premiership teams who were trying to get selected for the national side, it was a widely held frustration at the time, particularly in the backs, that Bath players seemed to be favoured even though the club hadn't actually won anything with their current crop of players.

I loved every day I spent at Bristol, and wouldn't change a thing, but I remember thinking at the time that if I'd have signed for Bath instead, when I was offered the opportunity at eighteen, I might have been in a different position. When you speak to youngsters playing the game now, those coming up through the schools, counties and representative sides, it is often just this – the perception of injustice and a loss of faith in the system – that turns so many capable players away from the game. If they are not picked for reasons they and their peers consider to be unjust, it very quickly turns them away from and against taking the established routes, and sadly many leave the game thinking that their path is blocked or that it's simply not to be.

Despite the results on the infamous 'Tour of Hell' in 1998, I genuinely thought I'd had a reasonable tour, though I am perhaps deluding myself a little. If nothing else, I'd played in a position I hadn't played in since my youth, and in an under-strength and outgunned team; if nothing else, I'd shown I had the bottle to play at that level. We were comprehensively outplayed and at number 10 you inevitably take some responsibility for the per-formances, but on coming home I thought, and was led to believe through some of the comments I received, that at the very least I had done myself no harm. That obviously wasn't the case. Radio silence, and the words wilderness and Moses spring to mind.

This was a time of reflection for me, one in which I did an enormous amount of soul-searching; it was, in fact, during this time that I learned most about myself. After the initial success of university, getting capped and, to the layman, living a dream, I cared so much about getting selected for the next level that moving to London and playing regularly for a big, successful club left me unfulfilled. I volunteered to help children with learning difficulties and special needs at the nearby school to fill the void; I trained relentlessly hard, more often than not being the last off the paddock, designed my own fitness schedule and learned everything

I could about nutrition, took pride in working harder than anyone else, experimented with different psychological approaches, performed well week in week out and still . . . nothing.

It's often said that you get what you deserve in life, that you reap what you sow, but at the time that didn't seem to me to be the case. I remember Lawrence Dallaglio, then captain of Wasps, making one of his famous speeches before a game down in Bath. He repeated the adage, making just that point, but I felt at the time that it didn't apply to me. I worked harder than my competitors; I definitely wanted success more than they did and in general played better. What Richard Rivett had taught me all those years before seemed no longer to be true. It is only now that I can see the value and truth in another old saying: patience is a virtue.

I've a theory about players, and though there is obviously the exception to every rule, the players that really succeed, those who are really mentally tough, have at some point in their lives been the ones who have suffered most. Muhammad Ali was once asked how he knew he was ready to fight. He said that if he was prepared to suffer more than his opponent then he would win. This is a powerful message and I think it holds true in many walks of life. It is often the odd kid at school who has the most determination to prove others wrong, the black sheep of the family who ends up achieving the most, the man who comes from nothing and earns his own money who will work hardest to keep it.

I'd been playing full-time professional rugby for over four years and now, with university life a thing of the past, with no other distractions at one of the top clubs in the country, without a sniff of international rugby I was unhappy and bored. Rugby was not challenging me enough; I needed to find something that did. I couldn't have put more into it, yet I felt that I was merely marking time. My life seemed to be passing me by and I wasn't achieving my potential. Also, judging by the response I was getting from the national selectors, it didn't look as if the situation was going to change.

The following telephone call – inevitable, of course, since the army had helped put me through university – could not therefore have been better timed. Cue the accounts department at Sandhurst.

'Are you joining us or can we have the bursary back, please?'

Now, obviously the boys teased me that I was the only man in history to be so tight as to join the army rather than pay back a student loan, but the reality was that, if I wasn't going to reach the top of my current career, then I would try to be top in another. Unfulfilled and not challenged enough intellectually since leaving university, with a few adjustments to my contract with Wasps, with flexible points of contact in each camp and with renewed enthusiasm, I agreed to take the Queen's shilling.

Chapter 5

Hurry Up and Wait – Sandhurst

Apart from the generation who lived through the Second World War, we had no direct family connections with the armed forces. This meant that I had little or no idea what I was about to let myself in for. The first day at the Royal Military Academy Sandhurst, or Camberley Comprehensive as it's more fondly known, was an eye-opener. You are sent a packing list before you arrive, the implication being that once you're there that's the last you'll see of civilisation until you retire. This list comprises: Polish, black (parade) × 1. Shoe, black, laced × 1. Shirt, formal × 2. Shirt, informal × 1. Suit, pin-stripe (obviously!) × 1. Starch × 1, Brasso × 2. Dinner jacket × 1. Toothpaste, soap and razor. . . . ???? Then I was welcomed to the second most baffling thing about military life – the language and the acronyms. Everyone seemed to talk in code – sit rep this, RV that, cracking on something else and standing by for what exactly?

If you then add the myriad ranks, regimental traditions and, not least, what people actually do, then to a comparative LLCSB (low-life civvie scumbag), it is more than a little perplexing from day one. Fortunately I wasn't the only one looking slightly lost as I arrived with a massive ironing board under my arm. Fairly quickly we all found a few kindred spirits as the shouting began. 'Cha-cha-cha' is apparently the same as 'Jack Borr Jack Borr', as is 'Ooff, Ight, Ooff Ight', most commonly known as 'Left, Right Left, Right'.

After dropping our luggage off, we were marched at double time from one department to another for all the necessary checks, signing our lives away and picking up the mountain of kit. Very quickly it became apparent that wearing a thick suit, shirt, tie and best brogues didn't exempt you from running with your kit from one place to the other. We stopped for an hour merely to practise screaming 'Punch' at the tops of our voices and to see who would be the first to break his foot stamping it into the ground.

Mealtimes were another pleasurable experience, with the entire intake having precisely three minutes to get in, get served, eat and be back out on parade. Having been brought up with two brothers who cleared your plate quicker than a plague of locusts if you rested your knife for so much as a nanosecond, I considered myself pretty well versed in speed eating, but this was a different level altogether – especially when you'd then get a bollocking for parading in bad order with food spilled down your front. I remember a couple of Old Etonians joking ruefully at the lack of time allowed for them to finish their genteel G&Ts at dinner; not what they had signed up for at all. Yes, it was hectic, hard but, on reflection, so much fun.

At Sandhurst the teaching staff tend to be on a two-year roster and those selected to educate Her Majesty's officers are of the highest possible calibre in the British armed forces, so that the very best of practices are taught and continued.

Drill, which is undertaken on ceremonial occasions, is a speciality of the Household Division, which comprises the regiments most often called upon to guard the royal household. Consequently the almost anal attention to detail was rigorously enforced. Although most armed forces throughout the world merely pay lip service to drill, it still forms the cornerstone of British basic training. It is actually of no relevance to the physical nature of modern warfare and, to be honest, never really floated my boat, but as the original means by which commanders were able to orchestrate their troops on the battlefield, its use is now more important in terms of personal discipline. That it takes discipline, personal pride in appearance and effort to become good at drill is unquestionably true, but, not having the willowy build of a 1920s cavalry officer – 'Chunk' was the nickname they affectionately screamed at me – I apparently couldn't put my arms down to my ribs properly. Next to me was my good friend Paul Adams. He was a genius on horseback, being a successful three-day eventer, but years of sitting bowlegged in the saddle hadn't been kind to his gait. He wasn't destined for the guards either, to the extent that other platoon sergeants used to come and watch him, staring in disbelief at the way he moved. Between the two of us it was quite a sight. Graceful it was not.

One of the inevitable consequences of doing so much drilling was that, once outside the gates of Sandhurst and back in the real world, walking alongside a friend you'd subconsciously find yourself falling into step, always a sure-fire way of identifying current cadets on the King's Road, complete with the obligatory stiff-collared shirt and chinos at weekends.

Once we had settled in we received a speech from our then company Sergeant Major, Terry Harman of the Welsh Guards. He was an enormously popular character with the men, charismatic, passionate and hyperactive. He sat the company down and spoke movingly about his own background, where he'd come from and how that related to us and the men we would eventually command, and gave us some informal advice about how best to negotiate the commissioning course. It was a welcome reprieve from the daily ranting and one comment in particular that made us all laugh, and raised spirits no end, was his advice on relationships. Remember that as a very senior NCO he'd seen most things that the British Army could throw at you, but the biggest issue, he claimed, was the pressure that a career in the army put on relationships and marriages. Having consoled many a soldier and officer over broken marriages, breakdowns and the relentless demands such a way of life created, he summarised it perfectly: 'Gentlemen. WOMEN . . . ARE . . . DRAMA.' Never has a truer word been spoken!

The first five weeks of the course are legendary in military circles, with no contact with the outside world, lots of the aforementioned hurrying from one place to another with no time to rest, a full curriculum of academic lessons, leadership theory and warfare studies to fit into a timetable that includes the rudimentaries of basic soldiering and, of course, physical conditioning. It was, needless to say, an exhausting process. I did, however, have special permission to train, and my first week coincided with playing for Wasps in the Tetley's Bitter Cup Final at Twickenham. Deprived of sleep, we had room inspection followed by ablutions and then drill for two hours before I was allowed to leave at around 10 a.m. Sorry, that's 1000 hours. Nigel Melville had the good sense to send me straight to bed rather than force me to sit through the tedium of various pre-match meetings at the Petersham Hotel in Richmond. I also slept on the coach to the game and for the first time in my life didn't bother going out to warm up, preferring instead to get some extra zeds with my kit bag as a pillow. We beat Northampton Saints 31–23 and a pass for the opening try was delivered to me within the first ten minutes that gave us a lead we never looked like relinquishing. It was a cracking day, Twickenham had been so full of colour and life, and afterwards the boys planned to head into the West End for a night on the razz. I, on the other hand, had been given permission to leave and play provided alcohol didn't pass my lips and I was back in the lines by 2000 hours. Though I felt I could have pushed these limitations, I didn't want to. I felt it was important to maintain my integrity so I kept my word and returned as planned.

As far as I can remember that was perhaps the only time I genuinely found it hard and asked myself if I was doing the right thing. I returned to my room, no one any the wiser as to what had happened that afternoon, all of them too busy with their own lives to realise where I'd been or what the team had done. I got a few texts from the Wasps boys rubbing my nose in it as they celebrated and I sat feeling a little lonely and a bit sorry for myself, bulling my George boots for the following day's chapel. The contrast between the euphoria of Twickenham and the gloom of barrack lines was challenging. After all, what was the point of working hard in life if you couldn't enjoy the good times? But the next day dawned bright and gave me the opportunity to challenge our unpopular platoon commander. It was his turn to inspect our rooms and there is a particular method to laying out one's drawers. I rather flippantly placed my new winner's medal at the centre of things. All I got was a flicker of annoyance across his features, confirmation of his absolute lack of humour or empathy. Conversely, while on parade CSM Harman gave me a sort of back-handed compliment in front of the whole company, acknowledging what we'd achieved by highlighting the fact he had video evidence that I hadn't polished my match boots properly! A knowing wink from the ex-SAS Commandant, the impressive Major General Denaro (RMAS's current boss), a man we all respected, was also a pertinent and much appreciated gesture.

They say that previous military experience is of no benefit on the commissioning course, but this simply isn't true. Character-wise perhaps not, but in terms of basic field admin, getting to grips with all those bloody names and who does what, it definitely helps. For me the biggest issue was which straps went where. Picture the scene: you're packing your kit with a list you're not sure is the 'official' one, or the one you actually need, that doesn't fit into a bag that isn't yours anyway, not knowing which item is which while getting shouted at to hurry up, outside in the dark, in the rain. Fortunately having a distinctly civilian set of mates, high on ability but low on the capacity to take themselves seriously, made for some comedy moments. Along with some of the more capable candidates I was always at hand with a sarcastic remark and always tried to see the funny side of any situation despite the serious nature of what we were ultimately training to do. This wasn't exactly the fastest way of winning over the most aggressive and uptight NCOs. Training was predominantly carried out with blank rounds and therefore, despite being absolutely fantastic in terms of strategy, logistics, administration and simulation, it wasn't the real thing and we knew it. It's interesting to note that those who did have a more enlightened attitude to training, who could get the job done at a canter and just as capably as anyone else but in a more relaxed manner, have all to my knowledge commanded with considerable aplomb and distinction in the live operational theatre, showing they have the ability to switch on when it really matters.

It did, though, open your eyes as to how much you could fit into one day if you got up with the sparrows. The days of afternoon naps, leisurely post-training meals and chats over coffee were now in the distant past. Having five minutes for a 'brew' was a rare luxury to be savoured; having a day off, combined with rugby training, simply didn't happen.

Whether it was the extra press I received for signing up or whether someone had seen that I could actually perform I will never know, but fairly soon after that Tetley's final in the summer of 2000 I was selected for the senior England tour to South Africa.

We were on exercise at the time, and therefore without comms to the outside world, when I was pulled aside from digging to be handed a mobile. Two minutes of excitement and elation later, it was heading back to the day job. Like all good military personnel the NCOs started divvying up all the kit I was to bring back before I'd even gone: 'Right then, so you'll keep T-shirts and bottoms, if I have shorts and tops . . .'

What all this did do was to introduce me to the delicate political complexities of our 'flexible' arrangement. The agreement of balancing full-time soldiering with full-time sport is fine in theory, with Nigel Melville and General Denaro and his chief of staff, Colonel Barry Fairman, giving the nod. However, the burden of adequately balancing the two so that I didn't compromise the quality of the course and, most importantly, did not lose the respect of my peers, in the practical sense fell to those slightly lower down the pecking order. That meant the NCOs and officers of the company, notably Colour Sergeant Cooper, CSM Harman, Captain Copsey and Major Hancock.

Apparently the army had found that it had missed a trick when it had been unwilling to compromise on full-time soldiering with Will Carling, therefore losing him completely, and so was eager not to repeat the same mistake with Tim Rodber. This had, however, created a level of resentment within the ranks and it was therefore important for me to strike the right balance, with the army having the final say. The game was now fully professional, which meant for some impressive time management and, of course, some helpful aides. Inevitably there were a few occasions when things clashed. I can think of poor Major Hancock who had, for understandable reasons, decided I couldn't miss a specific 'tute' (lesson) to play an away game in the Heineken Cup. Knowing full well that Melville would simply telephone Denaro, it was some-what embarrassing for both of us when he came back two hours later to tell me that I should now pack my kit to leave. Such a situation occurred a few times, to the great amusement of the platoon sergeants, who would congregate outside the office making bets on whether I'd end up in camouflage or match kit.

The key factors were that I could miss academic lessons as long as I passed the same exams and course work as the others. Time on the ranges was flexible if it was just practice, but obviously I couldn't miss the initial tuition of weapons handling. What they wouldn't compromise on was the need to prove yourself, whether physically or mentally, when in positions of leadership but most importantly in the field and in combat.

Sandhurst's motto is 'Serve to lead' but this was often adjusted to 'Swerve to lead' as generally, if you weren't the centre of attention, you were doing just fine.

The tour of South Africa was a goer for me and more than anything it made me realise how pampered the life of a professional sportsman is in comparison to the army. South Africa is almost certainly my favourite touring destination and it was probably the last of the 'proper' rugby tours. It culminated with a proper court session with Judge Jason Leonard presiding, Simon Shaw and Martin Johnson the enforcers and the completely silent Andrew Sheridan working for the defence. At the start of the tour Clive Woodward, always a believer in segregating tour squads, told us, the 'mid-week' team, in no uncertain terms that our job was to stay out of the way of the test team. After he handed Ben Clarke the RFU credit card, we did just that. It was a cracking time, pretty much the most fun on a 'professional' tour I'd yet had, which in the modern day with strict itineraries and accountability is rare. We actually managed to get out to the country, taking in safaris, schools, boozy bonding sessions and, the most memorable time for me, coaching at a club in Soweto township. The mid-week team were also unbeaten, playing some brilliant rugby against proper Afrikaans tough boys. Andrew Sheridan had just broken on to the scene; a bright but quiet man with the nickname Mongo, his strength was legendary. I remember one day when we headed for a weights session at a typical 'roiders' gym awash with testosterone. In such theatres of machismo the amount of plates on the bar is of paramount importance. It was with some amusement then that we clocked the appreciation and amazement of the locals witnessing Mongo's workout. Not only that, but you would have thought that in the professional age, and at international level, the game would have moved on from Under 10s where the tactic was simply 'Give it to the big lad'. Not here: it worked just fine, thanks very much. 'Right then, Sherry, you're going to get the ball from ten and run that way. The rest of you get with him for an offload. Any questions?'

One particular game, against Gauteng Falcons, saw some genuinely gruesome violence, with Darren Garforth suffering some horrendous bruising around his eye. This was South African referee Jonathan Kaplan's first senior game in charge, one in which he felt compelled, wrongly in my opinion, to sin-bin me for an alleged late tackle. Priding myself on a decent level of self-discipline, this was my second ever yellow card, so on the flight home I ranted about the injustice to the lady sitting next to me, who had, in fact, asked me about the ref. Being so caught up in the subject, stupidly I didn't read the signals and only on leaving the plane back in Johannesburg did she inform me that she was in fact Mrs Kaplan, Jonathan's mum.

Let it be said that by and large refereeing is a thankless task! Apart from providing a means of employment, why would you give up your spare time to be abused, hated, shouted at and told that you're wrong? After one particularly belligerent performance by Steve Lander, it was suggested that he'd behaved like that because nobody turned up to his twenty-first birthday party. In my opinion the same qualities that tend to make a good referee also make for a good bloke. Like coaches and players, referees do make mistakes – they wouldn't be human if they didn't – but provided they are consistent (or at least give the impression that they are), fair, are not biased and, most importantly, don't have a big ego, in general they tend to be respected and liked. On occasions, of course, they need to lay down the law, but balancing that with approachability is key. There are some cracking refs in the northern hemisphere and the likes of Derek Bevan, Clive Norling, Ed Morrison and Alain Rolland from the older crowd spring to mind. Wayne Barnes, the new boy on the block and a part-time barrister, is I think exceptional. It's said that the sign of a good referee is that you don't notice him. The aim of the referee should be to let the game flow, with it more or less reffing itself.

There are characters among referees, just as there are among players, and to hear Tony Spreadbury shouting '*Joue, joue*', or, to the claim, 'Ref, that went over', 'No, it didn't, you've scored enough already . . . play on!' always made me smile, although I always knew we were in for some audacious 'advantage' play whenever Spreaders was involved.

A sign of how rugby is modernising, and moving away from the traditional macho and homophobic stereotype of the game, was when the very good Welsh referee Nigel Owens felt comfortable enough in May 2007 to announce that he was gay. No one could care less what he does in his private life as long as he does a decent job on the field. The only remark you hear from the sidelines that gets a slight chuckle is 'the ref's bent!'.

On the subject of homosexuality, I love the story that Barrie McDermott tells in his book *Made for Rugby* about the Australian rugby league legend Ian Roberts, who came out publicly in 1995. Wayne Bennett, the well-known Australian league coach, was once asked about Roberts' sexuality. Hard as nails, Bennett replied, 'Well, if they are all like that, I'll have a team of them, please.' After a game, and the boys were having a few beers, Barrie, slightly pissed, having just received a couple of drinks from

Roberts, said, 'Eh, Robbo, you've bought me these drinks, right? Does that, like, mean you're going to try 'n' shag me or som'ing?' Everyone was burying their heads in their hands with embarrassment until Ian Roberts replied, 'Bazza, mate, I'm not being funny, but you're really not my type.' The conversation soon changed direction but McDermott, now wondering what was wrong with him, describes in the book how, within moments of being worried that a teammate might be trying to shag him, had then gone to being upset that he wouldn't.

Back in South Africa the test-match lads played a heroic first test, fiercely competitive, hugely physical and only missed narrowly winning the series 2–0 when a ball bounced unkindly for Tim Stimpson. They did though have five days after the final test when Clive disappeared and the shackles came off.

On a personal note, I'd been really pleased with my performances and receiving some very positive feedback from Phil Larder (former rugby league defence coach) and Dave Alred (kicking coach). I went back home happy that two months of borstal hadn't done me too much harm.

The fitness required by one of our soldiers is fundamentally different from that of the modern professional rugby player. Rugby is a stop-start game of maximum bursts, and though it lasts for eighty minutes involves a variety of physical demands. Military fitness, though, is also varied, and relies far more on endurance and being generally competent in other areas.

An analysis of rugby will show it to be a combination of power, strength, and speed anaerobic capacity – that is, the ability of your muscles to maintain their function with high levels of lactic acid, aerobically in that you will be moving continually despite breaks in play, the ability to recover quickly and repeatedly over the full eighty minutes – and endurance; but most significantly – and something it is always difficult to measure or replicate – the physical drain mauling, grappling and tackling huge men takes out of you. People often say that you can give an opposing team the runaround if you're more mobile than them. This may be the case, but actually it is the constant hitting the ground, taking contact and getting up again that really saps your strength. If anyone needs convincing of this, try getting your best mate, brother or even local nightclub bouncer (often the closest in size to some of the behemoths who currently stalk the rugby world) to take you on in a basic bit of wrestling, followed by fifty-metre shuttles, with a few sprints chucked in and then the obligatory rolling on the floor with someone kicking you for good measure.

Comparing one type of fitness to another is not a case of one being harder; it's just what you get used to. Your most basic soldier is required to be able to carry a fair bit of weight across any type of terrain in any conditions, from one point to another, in addition to being a decent all-rounder and able to adapt to most environments. In general this contrasts with the American soldier who spends far more time in the gym lifting weights, getting 'houh' or 'massive' as we more eloquently describe it. On exercises, they are more often than not dropped and picked up, with no need for the ability to travel long distances on foot. That's why on exchanges we just put weight on their backs and run their arses off.

Training for both the army and international rugby was obviously counterproductive on occasions, such as when a ten-kilometre march and shoot was followed by two hours' training at Bisham Abbey with England, but at the time it was a great exercise in just switching the mind off to things you couldn't control, learning not to worry about the unchangeable and simply 'crack on'.

The first term at Sandhurst encompasses basic training, learning the fundamentals of soldiering – and digging, for three days and three nights, non-stop, nothing else. If you really want to have your nose rubbed in it and be reminded of the suave sophistication of a fighter pilot compared with an ordinary infantry soldier, try doing this exercise in Thetford, Norfolk, next to the USAAF and RAF bases. The fast jets with their flashing lights and *Top Gun* feel kept cruising over, filling us bog-standard infantry with envy as we navvied away at flint and stone. Cosmic!

Terms two and three are somewhat more relaxed, although that word isn't perhaps entirely appropriate. The basic training has been done and the course moves on to more intrinsic elements of leadership and structure. More emphasis is placed on you sorting yourself out and being in the right place at the right time, the idea being that you're given more slack with which you can either prosper or hang yourself.

Wasps had started their season again and I'd bought a swish new flat on the Thames. Essentially while you were in camp, as long as you attended the lessons and got your work done properly you were 'free' in your spare time. I'd therefore mostly stay up in town, condition at Twickenham en route, parade at 0700, attend classes, leave for Wasps training mid-afternoon at Bisham, back to camp, finish lectures, skills work on the astro at 2000, prepare kit and coursework before heading back to town and a welcome bed.

During the whole year at Sandhurst I only managed to miss one game for Wasps, when we had our final two-week exercise in Cyprus; it is more a testament to the hard work of Burma Company's staff and some helpful mates than anything else. We still remain close and in decent officer style have established our own gents' club in honour of the company's name.

Once commissioned into the Royal Artillery, I faced the next few months on the young officers' course down at Larkhill, near Salisbury in Wiltshire. It became increasingly apparent to me that, with the fires of interest reignited at international level, doing a 'proper' job as a young army officer was becoming more and more difficult. One tiny example of this was with regimental selection. Being someone who enjoyed keeping fit and the hands-on challenge of command, I favoured, and had been accepted into, the airborne division of the Royal Artillery – 7 Para RHA, the artillery unit of the rapid reaction 16th Air Assault Brigade. Yet the triviality of not having compatible insurance even to start Pegasus Company (P Company) or my jumps was the first of many unnegotiable hurdles I encountered. 7 Para, a proud and successful regiment with a strong sporting tradition, quite rightly wanted me to work for them, but Wasps, as my main employer, were unwilling to accept this since parachuting would bring further physical risks into my life.

Our commanding officer, Major Gajor, a keen sports fan and an educated cricketer himself, understood the conundrum and on paper came up with the perfect compromise. 16 Regiment would be happy for me to fulfil all my rugby commitments and would be entirely flexible to my needs. This sounded great, but in all honesty it just didn't sit right with me. Logically, I should have bitten their arm off at such an offer.

Something, however, was still niggling me. I knew I could hold my head high, aware that I'd passed the same tests and exercises that everyone else had to achieve the correct standard in order to become an officer, but I just couldn't feel comfortable taking the same pay and rank as my friends and peers who would be dodging bullets while I swanned about west London playing rugby.

It would've been different if I was just going to play club rugby. In that case I could have stayed involved with the regiment on my days off, kept up with the social life where possible, and, most importantly, had a few months off every year during the off season to go on operational tours and do the job I'd been paid and trained to do. But if you accounted for summer tours, international call-ups and any pre-season then the scope for doing something meaningful and worthwhile simply did not exist.

The whole conundrum taught me one of the best lessons of my life. I've already said that to be as good as you can be at something you have to make sacrifices. These can come in many different shapes and sizes. Often, people want to achieve many different goals in life, but to become special at something you have to specialise. That means giving up other goals, dreams and aspirations. To me, it meant deciding between army and rugby. So over a few beers I sat my best mates down. Their response was unequivocal.

'Josh, are you stupid?'

'You're f**king mad!'

'No brainer, old boy.'

To a man they agreed that they'd all give their right arm for the ability to play for England and, with the opportunity of playing in the World Cup on the horizon, I resigned my commission the next morning.

Chapter 6

Getting Noticed

ON LEAVING THE ARMY after almost two years I didn't want to
go back to the same state of mental paralysis I'd been in
before and so I signed up for a part-time law degree at the College
of Law in central London (I eventually completed the course in
2005). Rugby was going well, although Wasps now found
themselves in a transitional phase. Nigel Melville was off to fresh
pastures, the back-up staff were in flux and Clive Woodward's
now successful businesslike management structure was filtering
down to all the top clubs and other international teams.

Despite my studies, I had the time to focus on rugby and nothing
else, and following on from the tour of South Africa I was
regularly selected for the national squad, although never for the
match twenty-two. I was one of the bag holders. As such, with
calls from the Sevens squads and my keenness to do something fun
and worthwhile, where possible I was allowed to travel the globe
on the Sevens circuit. Joe Lydon was team manager, Mike Friday
team coach, Terry Newsome physio and John Elliot the support
staff. An extremely likeable but also talented group, they created
a dynamic but enjoyable environment in which the players

could flourish. For the first time ever England began to compete with the more established Sevens powerhouses of New Zealand and Fiji.

Sevens, by its very nature, is to my mind the best 'blooding' opportunity for any aspiring player and an equally good one for 'rehabilitating' older players. The number of players who have graduated through this system to the senior national teams over the past few years confirms that.

Good players enjoy Sevens, limited players don't. The extra time and room allows for people to get exposed more, or demonstrate their ability. In comparison to the constant pressure of league rugby and its somewhat attritional nature, Sevens provides a brilliant vehicle as a finishing school to build the playing confidence of youngsters attempting to make the transition to the next level, working on fitness, skills, special awareness, defensive accountability and creativity, not to mention the implications for mental preparation. For the older player, I describe the Sevens circuit as The Priory of the rugby world where players who've come off the rails a bit can get their keenness, enthusiasm, confidence or downright potency back after a period of staleness within their domestic competitions.

Most significantly, the nature of the tournaments, with their quick turnaround game structure, gives players time for great mental preparation. At Fifteens there's usually a week to prepare and thus, by the time the game comes around, the build-up and nerves can sometimes have an inhibitive effect on a player as he 'thinks too much', especially as in some positions players can go for long periods without being involved. In Sevens, because of the stop-start, exhausting, all-involving nature, you are forced to just 'do', coolly concentrating purely on performance without the need for any big emotional build-up in what is fundamentally, as in most sports, a game of reactions.

Culturally, Sevens are great, too. Perhaps harder to play with a family at home, but with the professional game preventing a lot of youngsters from completing the otherwise obligatory year of travelling after school, it's a great way to see parts of the world whose paths aren't as well worn on the rugby map. In one year I had my passport stamped in China, Chile, Argentina, Australia, Hong Kong and, of course, Manchester for the Commonwealth Games.

As I've said, with a history-teaching mother and a Welsh bloodline, the implications of colonialism, imperialism and Celtic subjugation had been drilled into me from the year dot and thus I had a reasonable grasp as to why we were coined in Mar del Plata (Argentina) and booed everywhere else. However, my greatest memory of that time, aside from the bikini world championships on Mar del Plata's beach, was being in the first England team ever to win the blue ribbon Sevens event in Hong Kong. Being full of expats its ground is also the only one you'll play at outside our green and pleasant land in which England are the crowd's favourite. After a successful build-up, with the crowd perhaps sensing that something historical was about to happen – but most significantly the front row of the south stand being sponsored by Spearmint Rhino – the atmosphere was amazing and we were keen to play our part. For anyone who enjoys watching sport, the south stand at the HK Sevens is perhaps the Mecca of rugby and should be on everyone's tick list.

We played Fiji in the final as the heavens opened. The greatest of all Sevens exponents, Waisale Serevi, captained their team but, being more used to the Pacific sunshine than the equivalent of a wet February in Acton, wasn't able to pull off his usual tricks. We were quite happy to kick and chase and let him try and run it from the muddy slop of his in-goal area. They pushed us close a couple of times, but a young Simpson-Daniel nabbed a hat-trick, Henry Paul found his league flair and Waisale, probably nearing his late seventies at that time, didn't quite have the legs to steal the game.

* * *

On my return, Wasps were still in a state of turbulence, failing to achieve their potential. Although qualifying for Europe each year, we weren't really in the hunt for trophies. Leicester swept all before them with Johnson, Back, Rowntree et al bagging two European cups and three domestic trophies. With a regular home crowd of over 17,000 and owning their own ground, Leicester had been the best club at negotiating the transitional period into professional rugby and, unlike many others, had successfully retained their character, didn't rely on one, single benefactor and with a mature and settled squad were best placed to perform on and off the field.

The England team were regularly performing now as New Zealand had more recently, dispatching any team before them at a canter, except in the really key games. Each time, however, England, having failed to perform in the World Cup in 1999, would also fall at the final hurdle, losing out on potential Grand Slams. It is well known that the mental strength that was so apparent in 2003 was born from the heartache of this period. Clive had really focused on beating the southern hemisphere teams and rightly judged himself against them. It appeared that it was going to be just a matter of time. The key period of maturity came during the autumn 2002 series when they beat New Zealand (31–28), Australia (32–31) and South Africa (53–3) in consecutive weeks.

Rather annoyingly those of us not in the main squad would get packed off from Pennyhill Park, near Bagshot, on a Tuesday or Wednesday after being a stunt cock for the senior boys for a couple of days, then head up to Mottram Hall in Cheshire to play for the As, on the understanding that if you played well for them, something might come of it. The reality was that most Premiership games were of a better standard and, regardless how you played, it didn't seem to make a blind bit of difference.

Without being cynical, everyone felt the same, but despite the situation we were all eager to impress, tried our hardest not to upset anyone and above all else, took care not to lose, as this wouldn't do our chances any good. So with a wry acceptance of the way things were, we established our routine stops on the M6 and abused the travel expenses.

Louise Ramsay was the incredibly efficient senior team manager and, despite also being a lovely family lady, her tap on the shoulder come Tuesday afternoon, signalling your separation from the main squad, was like that of the Grim Reaper standing over you telling you that your time was up.

After repeatedly being ignored, with no feedback or answers, I resigned myself to the fact that I just wouldn't get a run in the side. Any information you did get was often sporadic, inconsistent, based on hearsay or simply just illogical. I wasn't the only one in this boat and so, though not satisfied with it, didn't allow myself to be too aggrieved about the situation. England were successful and playing entertaining winning rugby, but I just wanted to be part of it. So, rather than let it consume me as it had done before, as my own harshest critic I focused on being accountable only to myself and to those I trusted, not to concern myself with the consequences of how I played, finding my own answers and, ultimately, on just taking enjoyment from doing something that I cared so deeply about.

Wasps continued to have a fallow period in terms of silverware, which probably didn't help my chances, but this was all about to change.

Chapter 7

Evolution

ENTER WARREN GATLAND and Shaun Edwards. Warren arrived in 2002, as the incoming director of rugby, and spent his first few weeks under the wing of Nigel Melville perusing, measuring things up and taking on board the chemistry, culture and the individuals who made up the club in his unassuming but far from insignificant manner. Nigel then moved on and what was to happen next would, in my opinion, be a major step in the development of the professional game.

When you look back at the milestones of the game, there have of course been enormous developments since the advent of professionalism in 1995. But sport, just as in business, has its structures and working practices. Those clubs that are most successful – that have the most efficient and organised working structures that enable their team to win and win again – will lead the field. Other clubs see just what makes the successful club work and so the practices spread as employees are poached, transferred and in a sense cross-pollinate – that is, until someone else comes in and changes those practices again for the better and takes the next step forward. Although it sounds a bit melodramatic, it is this evolution in the game that I believe will in time mark the point when club rugby, in playing standards at least, was on a par with and would ultimately supersede the international game.

The seven years in the lead-up to Warren Gatland joining Wasps as coach were marked by a seismic shift in the way rugby was managed and perceived by the public. The first year of professionalism was 1995, with all the excitement and potential of the commercial opportunities it offered. The game of rugby was now a major sport with the ability to unite and energise, to help the birth of a new, apartheid-free South Africa; and, finally, it was transformed into a game in which the watchword was athleticism, symbolised by a certain Jonah Lomu. In 1997, New Zealand demonstrated the future of the game, the All Blacks of that year being one of the most complete teams ever to take the field, mixing the more traditional dark arts – the scrums, mauls, lineouts, rucks etc. – with a ruthless intensity and level of skill unmatched by any other. In 2000, Clive Woodward finally got all his ducks in a row, embracing the best of other sports but most notably the NFL, in which business-style accountability was adopted within an extended management and coaching entourage. In 2002–3, on the back of the euphoria, financial wealth and confidence of the English game, the club game stood up and demanded to be counted.

When I started playing professional rugby in 1995–6 most teams had a coach, a fitness coach and then a manager who doubled up as team administration and kit man. An assistant coach was a luxurious optional extra. Under Clive, his near obsessive drive for perfection led to a fundamental change in the management and coaching approach to the professional game, with every department having an accountable line manager. There were now attack, defence, skills, set-piece, front five, fitness and vision coaches with a back-up team of refereeing, legal advisers and analysis support both on and off the field, not to mention team administration, cook, press and eventually PR and, of course the tsar himself! However, as I'm sure Francis Baron, the RFU Chief Executive, would testify, this costs lots of money and few unions, let alone clubs, could afford such resources.

Some people criticised Clive, particularly after the 2005 Lions tour to New Zealand in which the autocratic style that had brought World Cup triumph failed to produce the required results. Undoubtedly Clive's philosophy had garnered little reward there, but he was to all intents and purposes the managing director (in a business sense) of the club. His strengths were always strategy, structure and leadership. He knew this and thus appointed people around him accordingly to deal with the hands-on elements of technical coaching. In essence his mantra was 'Never leave a stone unturned', that in every aspect the 1 per cent mattered. He was ruthless in demanding similar standards in those around him and you've got to admire and praise a man of such professionalism, drive and principle – as I did publicly at the time, even though it didn't go down with my playing peers as a particularly cool thing to do.

That's not to say, of course, that an individual doesn't make mistakes or, more significantly, cannot be let down by those around him. With such vision also came some fairly eccentric ideas. Once he mentioned buying some jet engines and setting them up around the pitch at Twickenham to act as wind turbines so that we could train and get used to playing in a gale. Logical perhaps, but unsurprisingly Rolls-Royce 747s don't come cheap and the groundsman wasn't exactly enamoured with the idea! Johnno (Martin Johnson) worked exceptionally well with Clive, never publicly (or even to the rest of us) showing any division or difference in opinion but, rather, worked as a decent safeguard against or filter for his more 'broad church' ideas. Regardless of whether he was right or wrong, under Clive, whether in success or failure, you unquestionably knew where you were going. A good analogy is that of a ship – you either jumped onboard and played by the rules, or you stayed in the water and swam on your own!

Clive's first few years in charge did throw up a few amusing tales, most of them involving the battle between his eternal quest for perfect preparation and Francis Baron's balance sheet. Not satisfied with the senior England team staying in the Cape Town Holiday Inn with the South African Under 21s and a few silver spoon gap-year students, and buoyed by the presence of the true 'chairman of selectors' (his wife, now Lady Jane), Clive told us to pack our kit as we were heading for the more opulent Royal Mount Nelson on his personal credit card. We all giggled with amusement as Clive threatened the bean counters that if they didn't pay for it he'd tell the press. Ironic, then, that as he challenged the status quo from the beginning, it was also, according to him, this financial wrangling that led to his eventual departure.

On more slender resources (as anyone who's visited Wasps' former Acton community centre will verify) Warren Gatland started to reshape the playing, management and coaching structure that initiated the most successful run in professional club rugby history. Shaun Edwards was his head coach and always the effervescent RSM. Warren brought on board Craig White, the fitness expert, from Wigan: he was brilliant, just the right blend, able to earn respect with his knowledge, designing the ideal itinerary and yet still being personable and approachable enough to be one of the boys. It was revolutionary having a fitness coach run the day-to-day timetable, determining when we worked hard, when we rested and how long we trained. It was a breath of fresh air and we never once trained for more than an hour. It brought an intensity to every session, as knowing right or wrong, good or bad, that you only had sixty, forty or even twenty minutes to get everything right, you'd get your head down. On reflection that helped your mental approach at game time. With such influence within the club, a deeply driven and on occasion aggressive streak and being rather small in stature, he was fondly compared with Kim Jong-Il of Korea. Craig White's influence on the entire Premiership is now huge. His apprentices or understudies have often gone on to head up other Premiership clubs and even unions, with Alan Ryan at London Irish, Mark Bitcombe doing the Scotland job and now Paul Stridgeon, the charismatic 'Bobby Bushay' as he is known, becoming Calvin Morriss's assistant with England. It is also of no small coincidence that during his brief spell at Leicester they won their only major trophy of recent times when they simply outpowered Gloucester in the Guinness Premiership final in 2007. After a comment that week which understandably favoured his current employers, you can imagine then that the team talk didn't need to consist of much before we beat them in the Heineken Cup final the following Saturday. Warren also cut out the dead wood and, as he has more recently with Wales, started to get the best from the talent we had.

Warren was a realist and knew what mattered to players without bombarding them with excessive paperwork, meetings and especially unnecessary box-ticking training. Less was certainly more. He advocated a running game and, as demonstrated, claimed that we could literally, with a superior level of fitness, run the other team off the field. When most other teams were more concerned with aesthetics, he championed a ferociously powerful and confrontational ball-carrying and retention game, a high-risk, high-reward, revolutionary style of blitz defence, but most significantly, along with Shaun, a mental approach that is in my experience unique and the key to the winning characteristic embodied by the players.

At Wasps, individuality was encouraged, unlike at some clubs where it seemed a certain mould was created or the perfect clone generated by one or two senior individuals, reinforced by the coaches: if your face didn't fit then you didn't fit either. At our place people were judged on their performance on the field alone, pure and simple. We may have been the collection of social misfits, waifs and strays that Warren described us as, but we certainly started performing on the pitch. Wasps invested enormously in the conditioning side with Craig White heading up the most impressive fitness structure I've known or heard of. He was fairly revolutionary himself, concentrating especially on power and strength, but making all the training game-related, of the utmost intensity and adding variety to what had gone before. His philosophy was that you could be as talented as you liked, but on the field if you didn't have the horsepower to match that ability then you couldn't do the job. Personally, I don't entirely agree with that mindset, believing that there is a decent balance to be had somewhere between being an Arnie lookalike and having the skills to create and manipulate space. But unquestionably it got results and locking the youngsters in the gym till they reached a certain size, strength and speed has been vindicated by the continuous production of top-quality players from our academy – Tom Rees and James Haskell to name but two. Also, aligned to his undoubted knowledge, ability, work ethic and excellent man management, Craig had the final say, even over the coaches, as to the preparation for players – making sessions shorter and sharper. With him he brought his Wigan mafiosi and therefore, along with inviting gap-year students to join his team and thus save costs, we had the biggest and most dynamic fitness team in the country.

Tony Hanks was on analysis. He was your archetypal rugby fan who just loved his job – essentially getting paid to watch the game and then giving more tempered and sympathetic feedback to players than the two main men. Lastly, Roger Knibbs headed up a tight but talented medical team.

Wasps now had an enormously effective team with a manager and leader in Warren, who would occasionally step in to impart his knowledge but delegated most of the time, leaving much of the coaching and beating of the club drum to Shaun.

The main advance in terms of the preparation and management of the rugby club in comparison to others, and the reason I am mentioning it here, was to do with the change in emphasis of how things were done and which areas took precedence.

As I've just said, the conditioning side was huge. Every effort and resource was put into making each individual as physically primed as possible for each game. For the most part this meant enormous amounts of hard work, but for some players it meant allowing them to do their own thing. When the likes of Rob Howley, Simon Shaw or Fraser Waters are preparing for a game, you don't need to flog them. If they didn't feel right to train then they wouldn't, and the coaches were happy to back their judgement, knowing that they had a whole career of performances behind them to justify that decision. This was in stark contrast to the international setups, or indeed to those of other clubs, where awards were given to the 'best trainers'. Our culture very quickly changed; you were given the responsibility of training if you felt it right to, but if you then didn't you needed to 'front up and deliver' in no uncertain terms on the field, no excuses. As Shaun would say, 'Eh, kid, I've been in the professional game for nineteen years and I've never seen medals given out after training.'

The message being given out was that the season was long so don't 'train like Tarzan then play like Jane'. It was a popular one with the players. And as a bonus, with the training sessions now shorter, sharper and thus more challenging, players actually wanted to train, wanted to feel part of things and to practise that mental switching on and off that they would need on the day of the game. Shaun and Warren's approach was very different from the established methods of training. Looking back on it, the encouragement to deliver when it mattered most, but to get away from rugby the rest of the time, suited us well, for the then new play-off system engendered a big-match mentality in our entire squad. London is a huge place and players come from all over to play and train. Obviously there were occasions when all the lads got together for some beers after a game or a social day out, but mostly after training they got away from the ground as quickly as possible and maintained a group of mates from different and more normal walks of life. This could sometimes be a disadvantage for those living alone in London, where not knowing anyone could be lonely and depressing, but in general it meant that the vast majority of the players had lives and interests outside rugby. Sometimes that's not a bad thing because it can act as a healthy stimulus so that you retain your enthusiasm and exuberance once back in the club environment.

It seemed too that every other club was trying to turn its players into all-singing, all-dancing, multi-talented individuals capable in every facet of the game. There was now a somewhat blunt know-your-role-and-stick-to-it attitude at Wasps, encouraging players to be aware of their strengths and weaknesses, to back themselves and to play to those strengths. Trevor Leota and Simon Shaw were the only lads in the front five allowed to ball-carry, the rest just being tasked with hitting rucks. All our back row were phenomenal athletes and with our backs we had plenty of go-forward options. Such a simple attitude was symbolised a few years later when Andy Robinson repeatedly ignored Oogie (Ayoola Erinle) for international duty, claiming that he didn't pass the ball enough for a centre. Shaun eventually took exception to this.

'Robbo, he's six foot four, seventeen stone, quick, no one likes tackling him and he's the best impact player in world rugby. Why do you want him to pass?' He had a fair point!

With regard to myself, although somewhat smaller in stature the message from Warren and Shaun was the same. The creative players were 9, 10 and 12; everyone else was employed for their athletic ability and so I was told in no uncertain terms to be more selfish. This can become a particularly contentious issue. When you watch a game on television it is impossible, short of turning off the sound, to remain entirely uninfluenced by the commentators. On the other hand, an international coach may perhaps be looking for a player to do certain things or, more often, vary their options. What Joe Public may not sometimes be aware of is that the player in question is merely doing what he's been told.

For example: 'Player X is so very predictable, he offers no threat and is just running into a wall of defenders each time' you'd hear Stuart Barnes say.

'Eh, kid, I don't care what it looks like, we're twenty points up, won the last five games in a row and till you start turning over ball, keep doing exactly the same, you're tying in three defenders each time making space elsewhere' is what people watching on TV wouldn't be able to hear the coach saying to his players!

On one occasion I came off the field slightly deflated. Though I'd run my arse off attempting to get involved in the game, I hadn't really touched the ball and felt I hadn't played my part. Without a word to me, in the next analysis session Warren highlighted six occasions in which my support running line had created the necessary diversion and interest to allow the actual ball carrier to make the line break. He then explained that one of (the legendary New Zealand winger) Joe Stanley's best ever games was when he never actually touched the ball, but created four tries by the lines that he ran in support. This is not the sort of stuff that ever gets mentioned or attracts headlines, but it opened all our eyes and proved that, by God, this was a guy who really knew his stuff.

Lastly, on a technical aspect – and apologies to any transient rugby fans reading this as for them it may be the equivalent of Greek classics to me – the advent of the blitz defence has been key to the winning of our last seven trophies. In comparison to the old-fashioned, safe but unremarkable drift defence, it still astounds me that the more high-risk but high-reward blitz defence has not been adopted by more teams. Drift defence can essentially be defined as the use of the sidelines as an extra defender. Thus, you shepherd the opposition in possession of the ball towards the sidelines. If you are of roughly similar speeds – apart, that is, from the obvious mismatch of a lumbering second row against a rapid winger – you show the opposition the outside. Either you force them into touch, and thus it's your ball, or alternatively the covering players can provide an extra line of defence. It is easier to defend against a team that tries to beat you on the outside than one that comes through the middle and thus disrupts your

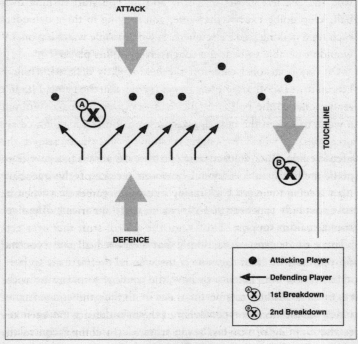

Drift defence

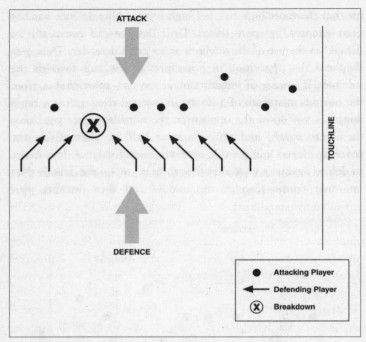

Blitz defence

defensive line. Blitz defence relies on an extremely aggressive line speed, a more confrontational heads-on tackling technique and either forcing the team back inside into positions where you have more numbers or where you can make more dominant offensive ground-making tackles.

To me this suggests quite simply that there are not many coaches and players who either genuinely understand the intrinsic technicalities of the blitz defence or have the courage to persevere with it in order to become competent at it. For all the emphasis in rugby circles on the need for controlling possession and winning first-phase ball, in 2004 we won the Heineken Cup and the Premiership title barely winning a lineout all game. Against Bath, the Leota–

Borthwick combination was one of the best ever seen, so much so that they were calling moves on our ball. On one occasion I asked Kingy what our backs' call was. He turned around with a knowing look: 'Josh . . . don't take the piss!'

The diagrams on the previous pages illustrate the basic mechanics but essentially it is the speed of the defensive line that backs itself against the skill and creative ability of the attacking line. It is not, however, the kind of tactic to win the statistics awards, which provides ample evidence for the doubters, because over a season you will leak more tries because of its high-risk nature. To perform it properly you need everyone to be on their metal, fired up and understanding their roles. Over the course of a season there will be lapses in concentration, different combinations in the midfield who will take a while to get used to each other, and some players will from time to time drop their intensity a fraction. But I can genuinely say that when operating properly, with everyone performing correctly, its system is unmatched. We have a saying at Wasps that defence wins championships. This was also true in the great Welsh sides of the seventies and in every World Cup winning side since the competition began. Though people remember and romanticise about attacking flair and creative genius, it is precisely the opposite of this, the ability to negate such magic, that, as history shows, wins. 'Attack sells tickets, defence wins games.'

As it is now under Geech (Ian McGeechan, Wasps' director of rugby), it was a player-run, work-hard, play-hard mentality at Wasps. If you had reached the required level of fitness, the management actively encouraged the lads to get away from rugby and celebrate whenever possible. Whether it's hearsay or not, in the 2008 Six Nations, after Wales had beaten Italy at home with a stunning display of running intensity, Warren explained that he didn't mind the boys going out, but told them to remember that they had a bigger, tougher game the following week: 'Lads, if you are to have a drink, just leave off the shots . . . use the pint glasses instead!'

Things aren't always rosy and as in any job there were bound to be issues, personal dissatisfaction or frustrations, but essentially the last few years at Wasps have been enjoyable, memorable and most of all bloody successful. The week after a loss for a sportsman can make you feel you're in the worst job in the world; it affects every part of your life and, inevitably, the people around you. Conversely, when you're winning it's the best job in the world. But even with our limited resources, with mould growing in the showers, blocked toilets, bottles of urine in reception (left there to be picked up for hydration testing), a waterlogged pitch and the depression of a cold, wet February, when it's good it can still be the best place in the world.

Chapter 8

The Moment

Very soon after Warren's arrival Wasps began to win and to win well on a regular basis. With the coming to fruition of the new conditioning and preparation ethos and structure we began to reap the rewards. As mentioned earlier, Warren and Sean championed the new blitz defence which inevitably had the odd teething problem, but once settled, with a regular midfield playing together week in, week out, the team soon started reaching its desired aim of disrupting and ultimately beating opponents.

None of our back line were leaving for international call-ups, which helped with our continuity except, of course, for our regular trips to Mottram Hall and the 'A' team. Every week, we were physically challenged to play in the way that we desired. It was torrid, exhausting but very enjoyable stuff and a complete change from what had gone on before. During the doldrums of English eighties rugby wingers were pretty much redundant, the game often resembling the Somme with sodden pitches and players 11 and 14 resembling corner flags more often than not – flapping in the wind with nothing to do. The game obviously moved on with the advent of professionalism but due to our rather inclement weather and wintry season, there are still periods when members of the outside backs and back three can find themselves with little to do.

The archetypal winger would wait out on the periphery for the ball, and it was his job just to finish off the scoring, but little else, and certainly none of the ugly stuff. Under Shaun and Warren, who understood that members of the back three were usually the best, or among the best, athletes in the team, huge work rates and involvement were demanded. Twenty ball carries a game was the goal, whether in close, out wide or up the middle. It was, frankly, exhausting stuff. Never before had I been in a team where people didn't want the ball because they had nothing left in the tank. However, going back to backing yourself against the opposition, and running them off their feet, we knew that if we pushed ourselves to the point beyond which the body didn't want to go, no team could live with us past sixty minutes. It must have been great to watch and it was brilliant and rewarding to play in. Players like and need to be challenged and this was certainly a challenge.

Technically it wasn't a case of running the opposition around, as that's not what drains a side; moving the ball from side to side may look impressive but it was the idea of going forward that ultimately mattered. Usually that meant physical confrontation. For the back-three players, though it might have been more tempting to save your legs for when you got the ball in space and thus have the freshness to exploit it properly, their philosophy was that if you didn't go balls-out from the start then that opportunity would probably never arise.

It always makes me chuckle when commentators who played in less dynamic times, when the touchline meant safety, state that 'Wasps have missed touch again', not appreciating – until someone has a quiet word with them some time later – that it is in fact a deliberate ploy to keep the ball in and thus increase the 'real' length of time that the ball is in play – provided you have backed your defence to make the necessary gains.

This whole approach was of course tempered by the accurate and correct decision-making needed to manage the game effectively, to close out and win tight matches. The ability to do the right thing at the right time needed wise heads, and we had two of the wisest in Rob Howley and Alex King. It is an area that can only be taught through experience and one I will touch on later but is one of the most vital but often overlooked and, more significantly, seldom coached parts of the game. The players people remember as great halfbacks are those who are not just talented performers in terms of their personal skills and ability but, more importantly, those who have great game management, decision-making and leadership characteristics.

I was settled, content and happy at the club with the rugby and the culture providing ample challenge and fulfilment, knowing that both the club and I were at last playing to our potential. I'd given up (and frankly stopped caring about) trying to impress the England hierarchy, at which point a strange thing happened.

The 2003 Six Nations had kicked off, England played Wales and France and again I'd joined the bag holders to depart on the Tuesday or Wednesday back to the club. England had won both games and though not sparkling had done enough to be viewed as firm favourites for the title. I went down to Cornwall as we didn't have a game and took a welcome mental break. I couldn't bring myself to watch the game, but one Sunday night in March I got the call that would change my life.

'Josh, it's Clive . . .'

'Errrr, hello,' I said guardedly, all the time wondering what he wanted, as Louise Ramsay usually confirmed you were needed for the squad sessions.

'Jason's picked up a knock . . . I want you to play full back next week against Italy. You OK with that?'

'Errrrrr ...' I said, shocked at the unexpected news, '... Absolutely.'

'This is your ONE and ONLY CHANCE! ... DON'T F**K UP ... see you tomorrow.'

... ah, bless, nice vote of confidence there then!

Ironically, the number one song in the charts at the time was Eminem's 'Lose Yourself', which includes the words 'one opportunity', so Clive's comments were particularly apt for me now that this one opportunity had been presented to me. This opportunity was what I'd left the army for – giving up a potential career which suited me and one that I had loved for a chance to play for my country. I was hugely excited, but knowing that I had only one stab at it was also a little intimidating. I remember thinking to myself about how I'd prepare throughout the week and the mindset I'd take on to the field. In order to 'seize the moment', did I have to be vocal, energetic and exuberant in training, liaise closely with the coaches, working studiously to impress, or did they prefer you to be mute and aloof?

By this time I had a very good grasp of who I was and what I was like. I had been out of favour for years with these people and every time I'd tried to get in contact with them my calls hadn't been returned and, what's more, I had been led to believe that I was neither popular nor valued. So I decided to employ the same approach that had been serving me well at Wasps and that had got me picked in the first place: to be myself. Having gone through years of inner turmoil about what I needed to do to impress, to avoid ruffling any feathers or just to 'fit in', I had become cynical and understandably untrusting of the system, to the point where I no longer cared. And now it was just this philosophy – of genuinely not caring about the England selection, what others thought of me and learning to judge myself and get my enjoyment purely from playing as well as I could, regardless of the shirt I wore – that had finally merited my inclusion. So I would nod politely when given advice, keep my own counsel and listen only to the people I trusted.

I tried to convince myself that I didn't care how I played and the consequences of it, but of course I did – hugely. The day before the game I ensured that I had a good night's kip and woke to my favourite sort of morning – a beautiful crisp winter's day. On such occasions your mind is all over the shop as you try desperately to be conscious of and prepared for the different stages of the game ahead. You walk down to breakfast and even the hotel staff, who realise it's a big day for you, say good morning in a tone that has an inquisitive 'how are you feeling?' edge to it.

Players in general tend to stick to what works for them and the morning of your biggest-ever game is not the time to start experimenting with different breakfasts. Marmite on toast with baked beans and a little egg or fish may sound fairly repulsive to most normal human beings, but it's worked well for me, and not being able to stomach much else before the game, it gives me my last proper meal before battle commences. I'll have a little snack about three hours before kick-off, but most of the fuel in your body is put in on the days preceding game day so I prefer to play just on the edge of hunger. After all, animals don't hunt on a full stomach!

I joined the early risers, who always seemed to include Richard Smith QC, our legal representative. After this meeting we developed a little routine, me with my rudimentary grasp of the judicial system talking through with him various points of law or a current case over an early-morning brew. Richard always tolerates my incessant babbling patiently and politely, perhaps realising that for me it's less a way to educate myself than a much-needed distraction from more pressing matters. This first breakfast with Richard was the last 'normal' conversation I'd have before heading back to my room and trying to get my head down again.

Clive, never one to leave things to chance, always insisted on having a morning meet, a quick get-together before more serious conversations were introduced. This used to make me laugh as, while the forwards would always do a few extra lineouts, the backs always wanted to go back to bed. At Wasps it was very much a case of 'switch on' when you needed to and don't pointlessly burn up lots of nervous energy beforehand. I didn't even want to think about the game at this stage. Trust me: I'd spent enough time in my life, and especially the last few years, dreaming of it, and the last thing I needed now was metaphorical premature ejaculation!

The routine goes like this. You meet in the Windsor Room at Pennyhill at about 12.30 in your tracksuits, having already packed, placed, checked and checked again that your bag is on the bus. Clive will say his last few words to an almost silent room and then everyone boards the bus deep in their own thoughts. It always amused me that being based down in Bagshot, thanks to our beloved health-and-safety execs and their concerns about noise pollution the national team, though accompanied by police outriders, couldn't put the sirens on to part the traffic on the M3 coming into town. As such the trip can often be painfully long; bearing in mind that you leave the hotel in a tense and anxious state, by the time you pull into the west car park at Twickenham the atmosphere can even become somewhat jovial. On that particular day I tried desperately not to think about the game so I read a book, not taking in a single word, and attempted to ignore the crowd when we arrived. In reality, arrival at the west car park is one of the best parts of the day. With the cheering crowds and the narrow tunnel, you could be forgiven for comparing it to the Colosseum as the towering stands of baying hordes celebrate your arrival. Perhaps a little too symbolic of the battle ahead, but for me, if they pulled down a cage behind you after you entered the darkness, it would be just as appropriate. At this point, there's no going back . . .

Everyone prepares for the game differently until the team get together approximately twenty-five minutes before kick-off. Jonny and the rest of the kickers will waste no time getting out to practise. They're looking to get the right 'feel' on their foot. About an hour before, after strapping my toes and anything else that is hurting at the time, I'll go out to get the feel of the turf, the way the wind feels for the high ball, and then physiologically start moving up the gears before the skill and technical elements are dealt with in the team warm-up. At this point all players understandably become quite preoccupied. Some days you run out and feel brilliant, full of energy, on others sluggish and knackered even with the best of preparations. There is obviously a lot of nervous energy being expended by each player in his own idiosyncratic way at this time as everyone attempts to enter the right physical and mental state. The less you think about it, the less you tend to worry, which at this stage is obviously a big advantage. This is why it's so important to have confidence in what you've done in the lead-up to the game. We'd had a pretty thorough week and as such I wanted to do as little as possible, knowing that it was all in the locker and it was just a case of bringing it out at kick-off.

The next stage is a presentation by the attack then the defensive coach prior to the warm-up, and then it's over to the captain in the last moments before kick-off. This is players only – the troops – the real blood-and-guts stuff that only people who've been there can truly appreciate. Whether it's England or an amateur team, the sentiments are usually the same and in fact often irrelevant, but it is to my mind the most sacred moment in sport. You then leave the changing room and are led out to the field and in that moment, leaving the tunnel, your dreams, aspirations, fears and joys flash through your mind. On the occasion of my first home English cap Clive's words reverberated in my head: 'One chance'.

It's easy to say that it was only Italy, but England were fantastic for the opening twenty. I bagged a brace of tries, one from sixty metres, and helped to set up a few more, and we won 40–5. Italy held on to the ball for huge periods in the second half and prevented a rout, but I was awarded man of the match and there were smiles all round.

Looking at it objectively, I'd had a very good game, but all that had happened was what I'd been saying for the last few years, both privately and publicly. The way the back three play is really only indicative of how the rest of the team is operating. If the front five are giving front-foot, or 'going-forward' ball, the big ball carriers can punch holes, generating fast ball for a creative midfield to put the fast back-three lads into space. Though this may seem like me trying to be modest, it genuinely isn't; the fact is that at that time playing in the back three for England, but especially at full back with the forwards we had and the Wilkinson/Greenwood axis, it wasn't hard to look good.

It may seem a little pretentious and ostentatious to quote poetry, but while others, and especially my family, were understandably fluttered with pride, I remember thinking about Kipling's poem 'If', most notably the bit about treating triumph and disaster both the same. So when we went to the post-match function at the Park Lane Hilton, with all the back slapping, hand shaking and new-found praise, I craved the company of the people I valued most and so slipped off quietly to have a few cheeky beers with those who'd got me to that performance in the first place – my mates.

What I hadn't realised was that these dinners, a terrible bore for players after an intense and exhausting test match, were not to be missed in any circumstances, with a three-line whip ensuring everyone attended. No-shows put a distinct cross next to your name and I of all people, having just got myself involved again, couldn't run the risk of upsetting anyone. So, not expecting the then President of the RFU to ask me to stand up and take an ovation from the 600 or so guests for my MOM award and my first Twickenham cap, I was of course not the flavour of the month with Clive as he growled angrily at my absence. Joe Worsley tried to cover up for me, bless him, claiming I was in the toilet when in fact I was in SW11 ramming turbo shandies down my neck!

The next morning Clive called. Nervously apologetic, I bluffed about the reasons for my early departure.

'Josh, I'm not bothered about the dinner. Are you OK? Well done yesterday. You're in again for next week.'

Having now stopped squirming, I then had my first frank, mature and constructive conversation with the boss of the English game in more than five years. I was in.

Chapter 9

Trophies

SINCE THAT CONVERSATION with Clive, at the time of writing I've played more times for England than any other player. The World Cup was of course on the horizon, and with England being given a genuinely realistic chance of winning it, the country's appetite for rugby grew as the event got closer.

The final game of the Six Nations that season, against Ireland in March, was at the oldest international rugby stadium in the world, Lansdowne Road. I'd watched games there every spring as a child, the Dublin docks and the Irish Sea invariably conjuring up the most challenging wind for any full back. I watched Scotland pepper Jim Staples one game, Paul Thorburn and then Tony Clement, favourites of mine who were made to look average, and now it was to be my turn. It's a lonely place at the back when you're waiting for a V-1 doodlebug to drop from the heavens, a team of marauding Celts baying for blood and 80,000 fans waiting for the mistake, but especially when it's blowing.

Ireland too had found winning ways and had scuppered England's plans two years before. They too were gunning for the

Grand Slam. Fortunately for me, my concerns about the weather were unfounded as the day was still and bathed in sunshine.

England had now become the best team in the world, playing the most challenging and creative football, but had missed out on trophies at the last by not reverting to a plan B when plan A didn't work. I think this was the match in which that ability to manipulate a game and close it out how you wanted became evident for the first time. Additionally, since Brian Ashton had stepped down as Clive's assistant the previous season, England, though still having the ability to play the Fancy Dan stuff, had just started to revert to a slightly more conservative mindset. While this of course brought trophies, having been blooded in the arts of the running game we could also now on a whim, or more specifically a furrowing of Johnno's brow, turn the tide by reverting to one of the more traditional English strengths. People look back and point to the pre-World Cup victory in Melbourne against Australia as England's best and peak performance. Though that may have been an incredible mental step towards convincing us that we could beat anyone, anywhere, and ultimately win the big one, I still consider the Ireland Grand Slam game as technically our best performance.

Ireland kept the ball for huge periods, moving us from one side to the other. Defending under Phil Larder's drift system at full back was exhausting as it meant repeatedly tracking the ball from one side of the pitch to the other and back again, and with the line held firm, and our lads defending as well as they did it also meant that, as according to the plan, I didn't have much tackling to do. The tackle count was over 95 per cent successful and had reached the world-class standards we had set ourselves. When we finally got the ball, after keeping it for so long without much reward I don't think Ireland had anything left in the tank. The analogy is a bit like the Ali/Foreman fight of 1974 when Foreman punched himself out. Thus, when we got the ball, with swift movement and accurate execution we ran in an impressive tally of tries.

A lot was made of Johnno's belligerence before the game when he refused to allow us to be moved prior to the national anthems. I'm sure it wasn't an intentional stand-off, but in the post-match analysis and in the press it was seen as a symbol that this team and its talisman were not to be pushed around.

It was England's first Grand Slam since the Carling era and though he had come so close on many occasions, it was also Clive's first major trophy as a coach.

After our victory we understandably got hideously drunk in the 'fair city' and the rest of the weekend is a complete blur. My only recollection is of being disappointed with myself that I couldn't match Jason Leonard's ability – to pick a pint glass up using just your lips and drink it in one without spilling a drop!

Going back to the club after an international was always pleasurable, with a slightly more relaxed environment. Wasps were in the second-tier European competition, having failed to qualify for the big one the year before, but we were also in the hunt for the Premiership title after successfully navigating the new-format play-off system.

I know there are many people who preferred the old system whereby the team at the top of the league at the end of the season were champions, and although I am of course slightly biased, having won it four times out of six under the new system, looking at it objectively it seems to me both logical and more equitable to retain the new format.

For a start, under the old system the season was often concluded in real terms as early as April. Rarely did the season go down to the wire. This meant that attendances at grounds and numbers watching declined towards the end of a season, at a time when pitches firm up and teams are capable of playing a more attractive and marketable style of game. Secondly, when players are not in the hunt for silverware and in the relative safety of mid-table, they tend to take their foot off the gas and mark time before their summer off. I've been in this situation and, frankly, all the lads end up focusing on how their 'guns' and 'abs' look for their Balearic beach holidays!

So economically it's good for the game when every team has something to play for right to the end. Sponsors also love the format in which they can generate an awful lot more interest, with the play-offs alone creating their own excitement and a fitting finale. For me this is an important factor: the end of the season should be a celebration with the two best teams going head to head with a cup final atmosphere about it. The champion's trophy should be handed over at Twickenham, the home of rugby, rather than Rotherham away in front of two men and a dog.

Lastly, and perhaps most significantly, you can't really claim that the old first-past-the-post system is equitable if you're playing club matches while the internationals are on. Some clubs are wealthier than others and thus the old system ensured that only the richest could maintain squads large enough and of suitable quality to succeed. While there is a salary cap, a widely regarded and positive aspect of professional club rugby (although it is not technically illegal to break it), this 'gentlemen's agreement' has in some ways safeguarded clubs against themselves by ensuring the steady, regulated and professional growth of the Premiership within its means. Thus with a certain wage cap, before the play-off system, clubs were forced to go for better value from their players – that is to sign players who wouldn't be going away on international duty. Invariably this meant the influx of a lot of former international foreign players, which in turn hindered the development of English talent – the consequences of which English football is currently suffering. Only last season (2007–8) Wasps, with limited resources and the smallest squad in the country, lost pretty much a full first team to the World Cup. We failed to win a game during this period and it therefore begs the question should one be penalised for contributing so much to the development of the national game?

The fact remains that along with a smattering of top-class foreign talent (which, by the way, it is brilliant to have, since the best players often introduce different practices, cultures, attitudes and are great to learn from) we want England's top clubs to play, continue to develop and finish English talent, something all the top clubs are currently doing frighteningly well.

I think the proof is in the pudding: the last two all-English finals at Twickenham have drawn world-record crowds, filled the stadium with life and energy and have been graced by two great sides going hammer and tongs at each other – the perfect advertisement for professional rugby.

Touching more on the rugby itself, and gradually moving off my soapbox, my first Premiership play-off (in the 2002–3) season was, though perhaps not the greatest match I've been involved in, probably the best and most complete club performance. Gloucester, as they did again last season, had led the table from the start. People often ask why Wasps always peak so perfectly in time for the play-offs. Among other more mundane reasons, it's down to the mental approach championed by Shaun Edwards that he took from his mentor, Wayne Bennett. The team that ultimately lifts the trophy starts to make its move five to six weeks before the end of the season; winning is obviously essential, but the focus is on intensity and quality of performance as the team needs to lift itself incrementally, building from one week to the next to the point whereby in the final it explodes into its season's best performance.

This has served us well, except that every year to date we have had a kick up the arse just when everything seemed to be going well. In 2003 we smashed everyone in the lead-up, but then lost to Quins at home the week before the play-offs; the next year was Saracens at home, then twice getting thumped by Leicester away and then, in May 2008, against Gloucester at home. It would be a blatant lie to say this is all part of the plan but within the club's philosophy of a steady build-up such hiccups have always acted as a springboard to achievement.

Gloucester, now under our former boss Nigel Melville and ex-Wasps captain Dean Ryan, and playing a wide-wide style game with three separate pods of players all season, had won plaudits and fans alike for their attractive qualities. Also with the likes of Andy Hazel, Jake Boer, Phil Vickery, Trevor Woodman, Olivier Azam and Alex Brown they had an abrasive pack worthy of the legendary club. However, the wide-wide game was designed to combat a drift defence that can, at worst, be passive on its line speed. The blitz therefore didn't do it many favours.

Without wishing to make him sound like a parrot, Shaun's favourite saying is 'to rest is to rust', which in part explains why his body's knackered, is far from pretty and why we keep the caffeine tablets away from him on match day! But there is a valid argument in suggesting that a team plays at its best when battle-hardened. Consequently, before our play-off final against them in 2003, while Gloucester wound down with two weeks off, we trained ferociously in the sun wearing bin liners to help us acclimatise to the potential heat of final day.

Twickenham is a huge pitch, and to play with such mobility and intensity everyone dropped two kilos as, once again, we intended to run them into submission. The day itself was horrendously hot but the coaches were smiling, knowing it would work in our favour. The game plan was simple – to start at full speed, keep the ball till we got either a penalty or a try and basically just see how long they could live with us.

That two weeks off hadn't done Gloucester any favours, particularly on such a hot day, and in the old-fashioned, heavy cotton shirts that absorb sweat the huge physical confrontations from the Azams and Vickerys, who'd been dishing it out all year, just didn't materialise as they couldn't cope with the intensity of our play. You can't tackle what you can't catch. When they did get the ball, the line speed of our front-line hitters – everyone except full back and scrum half – was so relentless and brutal it was demoralising for them.

That day, Stuart Abbott stood out for me, impishly jinking and unlocking a flailing and lethargic defence; Paul Volley too, a typically horrible, awkward and uncompromising open-side flanker who would die for you before giving up. Both men epitomised the competitive drive of the team.

It was a style of rugby that was challenging, involving and exhausting to play, but the result was so much fun, it was fulfilling and, most significantly, successful. Encouraged by the management team's work hard, play hard ethic, we believed in celebrating our victories accordingly. They were happy times and along with the England team winning trophies and accolades, and with the big one on the horizon, everything looked bright.

On the matter of celebrations, the Gloucester support had outnumbered Wasps by, I'm guessing, five to one, the loyal members in black and gold consisting of an awful lot of players' family and friends. Twickenham affords a cracking day out in the car park, particularly on hot summer days where everyone picnics and boozes in mutual enjoyment. After games, and particularly on such end-of-season occasions, professionalism understandably goes out of the window and so, keen to be with those closest to you, you get out and join in the fun as soon as you can. Having run myself to a standstill that day, and ingested the obligatory champagne in the bath, I went out to the car park to find no food or fluid left. As a long-time ambassador of Maximuscle nutritional supplements and a physiology student to boot, I was aware that crisps and peanuts weren't exactly the best things for rehydrating in 32 degrees of heat, and so the next thing I knew some pre-pubescent, part-time St John Ambulance volunteer was wafting diesel fumes in my face after I'd had a big sugar crash and fainted!

* * *

Above left: My first birthday in Kenya, hence the sun tan. Obviously the table manners haven't changed.

Above right: Tom (left), Edward (right) and I sledging in Norfolk. A happy time and a rare moment of brotherly love!

Left: Me and Tom in our obligatory Welsh kits. The future international half-backs-in-waiting.

The Chiltern under 10s team, with our coach Richard Rivett, before a game judging by how clean we are. I'm at the front, second from left.

My eighteenth birthday party at home with the family.

Me and my friend DJ outside the Wills Memorial Building in Bristol for our graduation. I was feeling a mixture of pride at having graduated and wearing my newly won 'internationals' tie and embarrassment at having had my hair forcibly shaven off.

DJ resembling Ron Atkinson, the third division football manager, Nick Druett in standard uni garb and myself in a borrowed boating blazer before a day at the Henley regatta in 1999. From Ascot to Goodwood, we went to every event of the summer season that year – an essential on any young man's check list.

Left: On exercise in Thetford in 2000. Officially the wettest year since records began, it was a rare treat to have sunshine.

Opposite: 'Last man standing' was the caption given to this picture that appeared in a newspaper after England's defeat by the All Blacks in 1998 at Eden Park, Auckland. Untrue, but the tour, although difficult, at least separated those who could from those who couldn't play at this level.

Below: Coaching in Soweto during the 2000 summer tour of South Africa. It was a brilliant tour and coaching in the townships was for me one of the highlights.

Cocked and made ready, but never released. Despite having had one swung at me, I've never thrown a punch on the field and at the time we couldn't afford to give away another penalty. This incident with Mat Rogers during the pre-World Cup tour preceded the famous tackle I made on him two minutes later.

DAVID ROGERS/GETTY IMAGES

Johnno and myself in Perth during the 2003 World Cup group stages.

DAVID ROGERS/GETTY IMAGES

Right: The most incredible moment of my life. Emotion overcame me as I was embraced by the very man who'd made me work so hard to achieve my dream. WILLIAM WEST/AFP/GETTY IMAGES

Below: Being a world champion feels pretty good! DAMIEN MEYER/AFP/GETTY IMAGES

22 November 2003, walking down the tunnel back to the privacy of the dressing room with the two greatest rugby leaders. For the first time in my life I felt like I could die happy and content. CHRISTOPHE SIMON/AFP/GETTY IMAGES

Me and Vanessa at a friend's wedding in 2006.

Above: Surfing in Cornwall.

Left: An all-too-rare moment of tranquillity. Away from the world, fast asleep with my beloved dog Olaf in St Agnes.

Left: A day out with the boys. A blissful switch-off from the rigours of rugby and city life with Olaf at his regal best and Wyn as a pup, misbehaving as usual.

The majority of the 2005 Lions test back line. We'd actually won that game, hence the smiles, which were rare on that tour!

DAVID ROGERS/GETTY IMAGES

With my parents at Buckingham palace receiving my MBE. Shawsy almost stepped on a corgi and the Queen was as patient as ever despite having the same conversation thirty times about the dogs.

Above: Keith and I on our trek to K2. Look carefully and you can see that I have facial oedema; losing fluid out of both ends didn't prevent me from enjoying the view from Concordia (which means 'high throne of the mountain gods') at the apex of the Baltoro Glacier – and of course caused great amusement for Keith on our summer 'holiday'.

Right: An 'after shot' showing the effects of a few weeks in the mountains.

Below: Ice climbing at K2 base camp.

Left: Posing in the Arabian Desert.

Opposite: A picture the public wouldn't usually see: the silence of an empty dressing room before a World Cup final. It is always a stirring moment when you walk through the doors and see your shirt and remember who has worn it before you.

Below: With my brothers and our uncle Alun. A stalwart of the Cwmllynfell rugby club, he – like his mother 'Mamgu' – is an example of kindness and generosity.

Left: Just after the final whistle of the 2007 quarter-final win against Australia. Gommars, my room mate, had always played second fiddle to the more influential Kyran Bracken and Matt Dawson but this was his 'moment'. Battered, bruised yet euphoric, he banished any demons and at long last produced his life's defining game.
REUTERS/EDDIE KEOGH

Above: Me and Prince William somewhat worse for wear after the 2007 final. Probably boring him senseless, I was carried out not long afterwards.

Scoring a try against Leicester in the 2008 grand final. There was a world record crowd at Twickenham with English rugby's greatest professional sides going head to head yet again. TOM JENKINS/GUARDIAN NEWS & MEDIA LTD 2008

Above: Me and Fraser in the bath at Twickenham with one of the two Heineken cups we'd won. I played with Fraser for thirteen years through university, and then at Bristol, Wasps and England. RICHARD LANE PHOTOGRAPHY

Left: Danny Cipriani cruelly missed out on the final in 2008, having played so well and done so much to get us there, so I ran the trophy over to him so that he felt part of the celebration. DAVID ROGERS/GETTY IMAGES

The jubilant and successful Wasps squad after the 2008 victory against our rivals. This was also Lawrence's last game. What a career and what a fitting way to say farewell. RICHARD LANE PHOTOGRAPHY

It's one of the best feelings as a player joining up with the England camp knowing that your club team has just delivered a great performance, won a trophy and, better still, beaten some of the boys you are about to go on tour with. You don't have to say anything or add to the swagger, but there's a quiet contentment that is just so sweet.

Meeting up for the summer tours is usually a bit of a ball ache, especially when the club lads are still celebrating. There is always a temptation to stay behind, get dressed up in silly clothes and have a proper 'Leo Sayer' at the end of season lash-up. However, this was World Cup year, I'd just got in the squad and was chomping at the bit over England's first ever chance to put one over the All Blacks and Aussies on their own soil.

We went to New Zealand and, surprise, surprise, it was raining. It didn't stop raining and then we left. I know in books such as this that it's sensible to be politically correct, to say nice things about everyone so that there are no reprisals and so that you don't provide ammunition for the opposition, but I've been there on six occasions and, in all honesty, though I've genuinely tried, I'm sad to say that it's the only country I haven't enjoyed. It is a country of unquestionable beauty, has a great outdoor lifestyle and is probably the greatest rugby nation in the world. Perhaps being there representing England is akin to a German footballer living in Liverpool, but on each occasion I, along with everyone else on the tour, end up counting down the days till we leave.

Most players enjoy training and playing, being fortunate enough to get paid to do something we love. But once training is done it's nice, and indeed healthy, to switch off from rugby and get away from it. That is nigh-on impossible in New Zealand. I sought out a friend of a friend in order to get some surfing in and see some of the coastline all British gap-year students rave so much about. Popping into the picturesque café afterwards I ran into a lady in her (let's say, to be kind) late seventies.

'Ah, hey!'

'Er, I'm sorry?'

'Truth, bro . . .'

' . . . ?!? . . .' (help!)

'What you think of Carlos, hey?'

'Sorry, Carlos . . .?'

'He's choice, cus!'

I suddenly understood she meant the flamboyant, unpredictable and maverick New Zealand fly half Carlos Spencer, who splits public opinion in New Zealand as Marmite does back at home – you either love him or hate him.

'Yes, he's very good,' I replied, 'a nightmare to play against, keeps you guessing all the time. I'm a big fan.'

'Bloody choice,' as she then departed.

It's a rugby-mad place but so are the west of Ireland, South Wales, the south-west of France, Australia and South Africa. This little example was a humorous and actually quite charming reflection of the place, but sadly the xenophobic parochialism generated by their press led to the most basic insults and abuse against the English team in most places, something you'd find associated more closely with the worst aspects of the round-ball sport than with the ethos we boast about in ours.

Despite this, I think the haka – the traditional war dance or challenge before battle of the representative cultures – and its Pacific Island equivalents are among the most entertaining and fantastic spectacles in sport. The sight of the haka in which a senior Maori will lead the others in the actions and words is brilliant to witness and though obviously stirring to perform is equally as motivating to face.

The first few minutes of a game can be enormously important. For all the words and speeches, what matters most is actions and nothing is more inspiring for everyone in the team than when one of your players demonstrates his intent with a bullocking run, or a huge hit. It sets the tone for others to follow. However, the game lasts for eighty minutes and a good start doesn't necessarily win the game. But if you can get an early lead, then you can affect the way the other team plays. If you go a decent number of points up, their initial tactics go out of the window since they may need to throw caution to the wind to catch up. If, then, you back your defence and discipline, you can make that work to your advantage. Back when Leicester went almost three years without losing a home game at Welford Road, they always used to play a lot of rugby in the first forty, often building an unassailable lead and then being particularly adept at shutting-up shop, playing a pressure game in the second half and living off the opposition's mistakes which they'd inevitably make playing a higher risk game trying to catch up. The last few Premiership finals have seen Wasps do something similar and even by just chipping away at a score-line, with our very aggressive style of defence we'd often pick up a try or two as a result of forced turnovers.

The mistake a lot of teams make, however, is to panic. Five minutes is a long, long time. I don't know the average time it takes to score a try but I'm sure it's probably not even thirty seconds. The key at certain crucial stages is to play tactically and astutely, and that may mean simply keeping hold of the ball or putting it in the stands. This is why it is so essential to have good on-field decision-makers and leadership.

Beating the All Blacks 15–13 in Wellington was, then, all the sweeter. It was a phenomenal physical effort with our 'old, slow and arthritic' pack, as it was described by the New Zealand press before the game, holding on at the end with only six of them on the field. After we beat them, the papers were then full of back-handed and faint praise, referring to 'white Orcs and Monsters', with more than a few petty insinuations about the use of steroids and cheating.

A funny incident occurred near the end of the game when Phil Pask, the team physiotherapist, ran on in a break in play. We'd heard the 'kit-kat' call, so one of the front five went down for a time-out and called for us to gather in for a quick heads-up. As Pasky ran on, he was getting instructions in his ear from the coaches high up in the stands. It was nice to see that they were even less composed than we were on the field as, down to thirteen men and with a defensive scrum, the advice came in as 'TACKLE!' . . . We almost fell over laughing.

On a more sombre note, during the final stages of the game Ali Williams tap danced on my head, resulting in me missing the final whistle while I was being stitched up by 'Big Bird' Simon Kemp, the England doctor. He, carrying some extra timber at the time, ran into the dressing room with me. Seeing him pumped full of adrenalin, gasping and sweating in his full Gore-Tex oversuit, I asked him to kindly get his breath back before jabbing needles in my head.

We cited Williams for the incident. However, the subsequent dismissal of that citation by the judicial panel left Clive more than annoyed. To his credit, he shunned cross-border niceties by sticking up for his players and making public his discontent. I was annoyed by the acquittal of Williams. The panel consisted of no northern hemisphere representatives, and, despite video footage showing Williams' boot going vertically down several times, three yards from the ball, it determined that (to quote their report) 'the contact with [my] head was inadvertent and incidental to Williams' endeavour to ruck the football in a situation where access to it was impeded by the position of the English players in the ruck' and concluded that his conduct was not foul play.

The fact that this incident involved me bears no reflection on my views of rugby's judiciary. Despite advances in the system since that dark episode, there remain huge disparities and inconsistencies with decisions made about citing incidents on the field of play. As a result, many players understandably have little faith in the system. Just three weeks after my own incident, Ali Williams received a seven-week ban. The person he punched on that occasion just happened to be the darling of New Zealand rugby, Richie McCaw.

The circumstances of the 2005 Lions first Test raised similar concerns. Brian O'Driscoll was spear-tackled in a fashion that might well have broken his neck rather than his shoulder. Despite the carefully presented complaints of the Lions, the commissioner appointed to the game refused to cite the New Zealand players who were apparently concerned. It was a bitter incident and left many questioning the system.

Fortunately no permanent damage was done either to Brian or to me. Rugby players being the sort of people they are generally prefer not to make a fuss and to move on. However, if Ali Williams' studs had been an inch to the left and in my eye, or Brian had broken his neck rather than his shoulder, then things might have been a bit different. Contact sports introduce the potential for huge complexities as to what is justifiably considered to be acceptable conduct as 'part of the game', and what is violent foul play beyond those acceptable boundaries. In taking the field, law and common sense both demand that players voluntarily assume a sensible degree of risk, including recognition that injury may well result from normal and accepted practice within the given sport. In rugby getting a clip, being punched, elbowed or stamped on your body is just part and parcel within these 'acceptable' boundaries. However, eye gouging, biting or head stamping, for instance, are not. The extreme foul play that can result in serious and permanent injury is considered amongst players to be a little naughty and, frankly, just not cricket. That sort of conduct can be deemed a criminal offence, and/or the subject of a complaint for compensatory damages in the civil courts. Had Brian or I been seriously injured, we may have been forced to resort to such measures.

Fortunately, the sad retreat to the courts is not something that has yet started to occur regularly at the top level of the game.

However, it is my feeling that in our increasingly litigious society, where there are still vast inconsistencies in the disciplinary process, with many players lacking faith in the 'in-house' legal process, it is inevitable that at some stage matters will escalate to a high-profile criminal or civil case. This has already begun to happen at junior level. A player was recently advised to press criminal charges after suffering a broken jaw. That particular case resulted in a GBH conviction and prison sentence for the offending player.

It is right that at least some are seeking to take large steps forward. That is why (the excellent) Richard Smith QC now rightly travels with the England team to oversee such matters. Sadly, it is my perception that – as with our soldiers in Iraq and Afghanistan – it will take a very serious and very public incident to occur before still more is done to perfect the rugby disciplinary process.

So, after I was stitched up, the doctor and I made our way back to an elated dressing room and, of course, resembling Pudsey Bear, sympathy was forthcoming from such sensitive and gracious souls! We'd tamed a talented and dangerous team, one in its relative infancy, admittedly, but we'd felt confident in pressing home that mental advantage we had of greater experience. Most significantly, we were winning when it mattered and on foreign soil. The trip had been worthwhile, but to complete the job we knew we had to beat Australia the following Saturday.

Australia was a different matter altogether. We were given a couple of days off and were told to go on the charm offensive by Clive and to follow Munster's lead in public self-deprecation – to talk up the opposition and talk down our own chances in public. It was, as Australia always seems to be, a fun, banter-filled week as we approached the last game of the season.

We met the night before the game for a quick motivational video, a couple of words from the boss and the lead players before a carbo-rich meal and sticky toffee pudding. Clive had warned us all week not to give them any ammunition and, having lived and worked in Oz, he knew how they operated.

'Guys, forget what I said, they've just annoyed me, call them what you like. They're all T**TS and I've just told them so in the press conference!'

Oh, brilliant. Cheers, boss, you're not the one playing tomorrow!

The game itself was quite the opposite of the previous week. Whereas Wellington had been a wet, stagnant, tactical arm wrestle, this took place at the amazing indoor Telstra Dome in Melbourne and as it was played on a dry, firm wicket was a show of fast-flowing athleticism with us scoring three tries to their one. We beat them 25–14.

Australia have always managed to produce quality, large, skilful backs and, being arguably the most comprehensive sports nation for their size of population, are perennial overachievers, with a competitive mental streak that runs through their whole sports culture. Although sometimes criticised back in Oz, in George Gregan they have had at their helm one of the best players ever to grace the rugby field. A gentleman and a ruthless competitor, he organises and co-ordinates their whole pattern and tempo, which makes him a main target whenever teams play Australia. Surprisingly, rugby union is only the fourth most popular sport in the country and thus, when you compare playing numbers to those in England, it speaks wonders for their system when you see how successful they have been.

Having said that, we'd beaten them the previous autumn and, especially in the forwards, fancied our chances of being able to impose our pattern and tempo on the game. Essentially, if you analyse England at the time, without getting too technical or drawing diagrams and flow charts, it involved playing with more width than the opposition. In simplest terms, though many may have seen the side-to-side play with lots of movement of the ball, the game was, is and always will be about going forward. To that end, by stretching a team from one side to another, it creates more space between defenders and thus more opportunities to use footwork, moves or plays to offset the tackler, allowing a 'dominant' ball carrying and forward momentum rather than the tackler being more able to win the collisions in more confined spaces. There are times when 'hard yards' are needed in confined spaces, in which your most powerful runners are used to carry ball. On such ball, you'll notice the Johnsons, Vickerys etc. trucking the ball up outside the number 12 – the plan being that by targeting this channel you avoid the roaming congestion of the opposition back row (usually aligned between the fly half and the break-down), and twenty stone travelling like that into smaller men when nothing else is on is just plain physics.

We created and finished some cracking tries that night illustrating, in comparison to the previous week, that this England team had the ability to play and win in any country.

At the time, the ARFU had been busy trying to recruit some converts from the more domestically popular but internationally less favoured rugby league. Lote Tuqiri, the huge winger-cum-centre, made his debut that day along with the charismatic Mat Rogers. They were both a handful and though we'd dominated the possession and points for most of the game, the impact of these fresh legs gave Australia a momentum that meant we weren't quite out of sight.

A lot has been made of our defence at that time and I'm often asked about my tackle on Mat Rogers a couple of minutes after a slight altercation had taken place.

Looking objectively at it, the press, television stations and the watching public pick one or two moments in a game that symbolise the overall result. These tend to give a rather sensation-alist picture of the entire game. Often it's the winning try, key turnover or an individual piece of creativity. In this case, because it took more than five minutes for play to resume, the TV channels had plenty of replays and so the tackle was seen as a fitting testimony to England's overall physical domination and aggres-siveness during that period.

My recollection of it was that Australia, with their impact players, had just about got their tails up. I had given Rogers a slight tug on his shirt, stopping him running the decent support line he was on, for which he turned around and swiped at me twice. Nothing malicious or indeed unjustified, but I did very much think I'd love to have a go. If they'd have got a penalty out of it and in all likelihood taken three points from the resulting lineout, they would only have been within one converted score of pulling level. And so, though it was enormously tempting to respond, I didn't.

Coincidentally, a minute later George Gregan lofted a real hospital pass to Rogers, shooting to the blind side. It could have been anyone exposing their ribs in such a fashion, but obviously with the last handbags incident still fresh in viewers' minds, for English fans at least it was just reward.

I have since swapped one of my World Cup final shirts with Mat and laughed about the incident over a beer, and being a keen but useless surfer myself, I can empathise with him and the pain it must be to have a surfboard specially made to suit someone with wonky ribs. He is a thoroughly decent chap and it would be remiss of me not to mention how commendably, some years later, he handled the issue of his father's death in such difficult circumstances – putting rugby and indeed public perceptions rightly into perspective.

So, both domestically and internationally we'd finished the season successfully lifting silverware, which meant a brief but action-packed holiday cattle ranching in Arizona and rafting in Colorado before the World Cup boot camp started at 'Pennyhell'.

Chapter 10

Socialist Republic of Woodwardville

I**T WAS IRONIC THAT** only three miles from the gates of the more famous Camberley Comprehensive the early mornings and shouting started again at Pennyhill Park. It was, though, great fun. With the genuine expectation and belief that we could win the big one in the back of our minds, it was a competitive but enjoyable and dynamic environment.

I was paired up with Andy Gomarsall as my roommate. To get by and retain a high level of morale over the next few months meant that we needed laughter and plenty of it. Gommars was pretty much the only person polite enough to laugh at my impressions of the coaches and in return he, being more technically minded, would always bring some DVDs of *The Office*. It meant that in between bouts of sweating your arse off, or getting beaten up, you would rush back for another snippet of the Brentmeister.

Theoretically you can get all the nutrition you need from a decent, healthy and varied diet. This is unquestionably true, especially when you're in a five-star hotel with full-time chefs cooking meals that have been especially formulated for training. However, when you're training up to five times a day, hotel food and indeed digesting the volume one needs, can become a bit of an effort. Luckily, by using recovery/meal-replacement products, we could spend more time in bed, safe in the knowledge that we were getting sufficient quality calories in without bloating ourselves out.

Under the watchful eye of Dave Reddin, the training was long, arduous and hard and the guys were all pumping personal bests in the gym. The average day consisted of 'vision' and 'awareness' coaching, rugby, fitness, weights, intermittent recovery and, of course, team meetings.

Dave Alred, simply the best kicking coach anywhere, a novel thinker and sometimes just plain perplexing, conjured up and devised various eclectic practices in the hope of improving our overall skills. However, rugby players being mostly somewhat cynical beasts, his theories and enthusiasm were on occasion challenged, particularly when he made disgruntled props, still scratching their bits, throw golf balls through hoops wearing eye patches, to the deafening sound of Dolly Parton at 7 a.m.!

With regard to props, our next-door neighbours in the hotel were Messrs Vickery and Woodman, the Cornish duo – the pride of the west and arguably the two best props in the world at the time. Humorous and endearing characters, it was always a comfort to see that, professionals or not, some things never change with props. At the time, with our diets regulated and nutrition pre-planned, anything bad for you had an incredibly high black-market value within camp. You could get up to £5 for a chocolate bar at the right moment, but the chances of anyone actually selling one were slight. A decent 'illegal' trade was carried out between the garage at the hotel's gates and the shared bedroom corridors, but it was a risky business to be seen walking in with a plastic bag full of goodies and so the clever ones tended to wait for the cover of darkness. The front-row boys were the godfathers of the economy, with Leonard, Vickery, Thompson et al controlling the main lines of exchange. Not surprisingly, being of rather chunky persuasions, Dave and the rest of his fitness team were soon in hot pursuit of such 'illegal' substances, so on occasion a mini-sweet shop would suddenly be shoved into your hands – much to the disapproval of Dave's enforcement brigade – so that you could take the rap for the fatties.

Vicks and Trevor Woodman would invariably take things a step further. Whereas Gommars and I were, very boringly, attempting to live the conscientious life, the fresh Surrey air wafting through the room amongst the protein bars and multivitamins, next door it was far more entertaining. On entering you'd find the most revered and respected props of the professional game lying naked in the dark, curtains drawn watching darts, scratching themselves, with ash trays, crisps, chocolate and biscuit wrappers strewn all over the place. It brought a smile to my face – props will be props!

'All men are equal' indeed. It's just that some are more equal than others! George Orwell's *Animal Farm* had a particular and amusing resonance in our build-up camp. You were either in Clive's circle of trust – known as the COT – or you most definitely weren't. The Johnsons, Dallaglios, Backs, Greenwoods etc. were all obviously within the circle, attending senior players' meetings and training strategy. You can't knock this because it unquestionably worked, but at the time it was the culture and the dynamics of the relationships that us mere minions, or 'infidels', found the funniest. I certainly wasn't going to challenge the structure, and to be honest never had a reason to do so. Having spent so long in the wilderness I'd learned to keep my counsel.

When writing a book of this nature there is a balance to be struck between remaining loyal to your teammates and others and telling the truth. While always attempting to get that balance right and without causing offence, I also like to try to explain some of the funnier side of events, some of the subtle components that make up life within an all-male environment.

Jonny Wilkinson was the heir to the throne, the Chosen One, and in imperial China would have been wearing yellow. Amiable, polite, conscientious, hard-working, self-effacing and brilliant, there simply isn't anything to dislike about Jonny. And being the man he is, he continually wanted to take part, continually wanted to excel. As you would with your top quarterback, however, Clive quite rightly sometimes had to safeguard him from the risk of injuring himself. To stand in for someone like this is known in the game as 'stunt cocking', a role that usually fell to Alex King. Despite being an elder statesman and having a gammy knee himself, Alex gamely stepped in for the full metal jacket bits.

On one occasion we were taking part in a structured, non-contact attack session, in which Alex was not stunt cocking. One side kept running further than it should and unsurprisingly, as the defensive side grew more frustrated, the physical level escalated. Jonny took the ball on and danced through a gap he'd made for himself. Jamie Noon, his clubmate at Newcastle, incensed by a telling-off dished out to him for something he hadn't been responsible for moments earlier, came out of nowhere and scythed him down with a textbook side-on tackle around the ankles.

Big mistake.

We all knew that touching the messiah, or worse still injuring him, especially if you weren't in the COT, was punishable by exclusion, death or even worse. Jonny was still down, the physios hurtled on and there was just that moment's pause when everyone backed callously away from Jamie knowing Clive's fuse was about to blow.

'Dave,' Clive yelled to Dave Reddin, 'KILL HIM!'

For the next ten minutes, Jamie Noon was tortured pitchside, getting put through a horrendous array of arduous physical tasks until Clive had calmed down, Jonny was back running about again and we'd stopped giggling.

One thing that Clive Woodward introduced in his business style of management was meetings. His aim was to get his coaches to illustrate, with the use of white boards, flip charts or whatever, the moves we were to put into practice, and you couldn't fault the diligence and clarity with which they set about their tasks. The process would start with video evidence or analysis of our play or of the opposition, depending on whether it was an attack or a defence-based session. The players would then suggest what they saw as needing to be worked on and this would be used as the basis for the next session, which would address and work on the flaws identified in the video.

It would be fair to say that some of the meetings were quite lengthy – but if nothing else this showed that the coaches had put a lot of hard work into their preparation. But players are like schoolchildren and they aren't particularly good at sitting quietly for long periods; they lose concentration and start to fidget. Asking Julian White and the rest of the front-row boys to sit through an hour and a half of back-three kick returns would be as testing as asking me to watch 150 scrums or lineouts.

Those lucky enough to have experienced the traditional Home Counties comforts of Pennyhill Park will be familiar with their rather ornate eighteenth-century chairs. These are beautiful to look at, if a little sturdy and functional. However, having recently suffered a bulging disc at lumbar level 4/5 in the recent tour of New Zealand, I found them bloody agony to sit on. So for three months, while I was trying to convince Clive I was fit and well for selection, the medical team suggested that to prevent continuous spasm I kept my knees below hip level, and so I spent most of the time in meetings and at dinnertime kneeling – I resembled Ruprecht from Steve Martin's *Dirty Rotten Scoundrels*!

* * *

The training was intense and tough but incredibly well structured, planned and orchestrated. Weekends were a welcome break in which everyone bomb-bursted away from captivity back to their wives and girlfriends. The Friday feeling was heightened when we had team Olympics – a series of team-based fitness competitions designed to knacker everyone just before a couple of days' rest and before it started all over again the following Monday morning.

These were fantastic for morale and inevitably, with places at stake and coaches to impress, the competitive edge created a balls-out work ethic, but not without throwing up the odd amusing moment.

The lads, always keen to cheat and to work together as much as they could, would agree to do the '400m' or 'pitch lap' in a big group, so that no one would be embarrassed. Inevitably, though, the temptation to impress overcame the collective spirit of agreement, with some Judas breaking for the line on the home straight.

The big boys in the front five were always paired up and, to save their joints from too much injury caused by pounding the track, spent a lot of time on the bikes and ergos. Despite his being one of the fittest pound-for-pound players in British rugby, it always seemed a little unfair to pit 5 foot 7 inch Andy Titterell against Johnson and Shaw at rowing.

There were also three warm-up games planned, one of which, it was believed, Clive and his French counterpart, Bernard Laporte, had agreed terms on. We were to send our second team to Marseilles and they would send theirs to Twickenham the following week.

The first of the three matches was against Wales at the Millennium Stadium on 23 August 2003. As far as selection goes, players get a pretty good idea as to the mindset of coaches by the team they pick and the combinations they announce. If, for example, you had

Dawson, Wilkinson and Greenwood in your back line, you pretty much knew, in the backs at least, that the team would go out with all guns blazing. Likewise, with Johnson, Back and Dallaglio alongside you in the forwards, this meant that you were in favour at that point.

In the Wales game, Clive selected a team of players to get a result, but who were also playing for squad places. It is a testament to the strength of the squad and its management at the time that this team, half of which probably wouldn't make the final thirty, would put fifty points on a first-choice Welsh team. Such games are make-or-break for some players; they know it and so does everyone else. Regardless of how well you trained, how impressive you'd been in the fitness camp, if you didn't deliver or impress when given even half a chance, it meant missing out on the magic thirty.

In most positions this usually meant that you only had one or two touches near the beginning of the game to create the overall impression that would ultimately determine your future involvement. Stakes were obviously high in the Wales game.

The two biggest casualties that day were Graham Rowntree and Alex King. A fellow Wasp, Alex, a popular and mature fly half, was second to none on the big stage and I still think his game management decision-making will play a big role in England's halfback development in the future. However, despite playing well, uncharacteristically he didn't have his most successful afternoon at goal kicking and, thanks also to a continuously troublesome knee, didn't make the cut.

Graham Rowntree, the hugely popular and respected prop who'd plied his trade for years at the coal face of Premiership rugby, who'd done all the training, ever impressing, ever enthusiastic, was left behind simply because the numbers didn't work. Clive and the coaches went for four props instead of five. There are always some people you feel particular sympathy for, and such a one is 'Wig' as he was such an all-round good guy. Clive's conversation with him must have been particularly difficult.

The whole camp then moved to the South of France in which 'the second string' was to play the strongest French team on a ground on which they'd never lost. I had been told I wouldn't be playing, but injuries to Dan Luger and James Simpson-Daniel meant that Ben Cohen and I started on the wings. It was a poor and frankly dull game, with the French having an incredibly suffocating rush defence. The stadium is fantastic, however, and the atmosphere on a warm summer's evening was only really matched by the excitement of the closing stages. We failed to convert a drop goal in the last minute and lost the game by one point. The most disappointing aspect was that it brought to an end England's unbeaten run, equalling South Africa's twenty-one games undefeated. However, records, though nice, are no more than that, and bearing in mind the location and the strength of the opposition, the feeling was that, while not playing well without the 'big guns', England were still in ominous form.

The home game the following week was a different matter. Without labouring the point, it was a dynamic and ruthless performance and HQ's fitting send-off to its realistic medal hopes.

Chapter 11

The World Cup

ABSOLUTELY NOTHING HAD BEEN left to chance. We'd even done a pre-tournament recce to the Gabba in Perth on the previous tour to 'visualise' what playing under the lights of an Aussie Rules pitch would be like.

Perth is a great place and certainly my favourite Australian city. It is very pretty, retaining some of the original Victorian colonial architecture, but is situated right on the coast with all the action of a beach lifestyle. The city seems to be big enough to allow you to do all the things you could wish, but still small enough to have its own identity and community – with the beautiful set enjoying themselves in its many bars and clubs.

We were based there for the group stages. Perth being a relatively small city, and with groups of rugby players tending to stand out somewhat from the crowd, it made for some rather embarrassing pre-game meetings. Back in 2000, while we were touring South Africa, the legendary film *Gladiator* had just been released. We saw it on the eve of a game, and when the lights went up in the auditorium at the end we found ourselves sitting next to the Springboks. Being a fairly blood-pumping flick, with the hostile looks exchanged at that point it's a wonder the game didn't kick-off a few hours earlier.

There were no such issues in 2003, but it was always amusing to give a knowing smile to any Samoans, Saffers and Georgians befriending the local surfer chicks.

There was the official welcome in which the local authorities put on the usual canapés, drinks and exchange of pleasantries. Indigenous Australian dancers did their stuff and we collected our World Cup caps. It struck me at the time, however, that the South Africans (the odd elder statesman aside) were being particularly cold. Perhaps we came over in the same way, but as our main rivals to win the group it seemed as though they'd been told to psych us out.

This theory was borne out by a 'behind scenes' session watched by a travelling army friend of mine. While we were in our build-up camp, the Saffers had been doing tackling practice with the faces of England players stuck on to the bags corresponding to their opposition number. Think *Rocky IV* where Rocky puts up photos of Ivan Drago and you get the idea. Whether or not this is true or just my pal trying to wind me up we'll never know; but as such closed sessions have become more common at top-level rugby, any watching supporters with cameras are most definitely not welcome.

Either way, you felt as though they had well and truly focused on that one game as their route to the final. The Samoans were as usual in good spirits, forever breaking into song, whereas the Georgians, all huge, their faces carved from granite, like the Uruguayans just seemed delighted to be there.

Our first game was against Georgia on 12 October, which we won comfortably 84–6. Without being patronising, they genuinely were bloody nails, making us work to the bitter end for everything we got. A few years earlier, I'd played against Georgia in a World Cup Sevens pre-tournament warm-up game and it struck me then that though the Berlin Wall may have fallen, these former Eastern Bloc soldiers weren't going to. Playing one-off 'take it up' rugby isn't normally associated with the traditional grace and aestheticism of international Sevens, but when all your players are over six foot four inches and seventeen stone they take some stopping.

We picked up a couple of injuries, most notably to Matt Dawson, for which Martin Wood, the charismatic former Wasps scrum half, had been called out on standby. Due to tournament rules, however, he wasn't allowed to stay with the team and thus occupied himself, as only Woody knew best, in a hotel down the road.

It struck me how well the Australians hosted the tournament. Though Western Australia is not a rugby hot spot, the streets were draped in bunting and there was a buzz about the forthcoming big game.

Despite the weather being hot and dry during the day, there was always dew on the grass by kick-off time under the lights. The game against South Africa on 18 October, which we won 25–6, was a bit of an arm wrestle, eventually being settled by Greenwood's charged-down try. However, as a back-three player the only thing I seem to remember is that it was quite disjointed, with neither side imposing a pattern for long periods, and that it was quite hard to get involved with the game.

Television, the press and public tend to sensationalise the points scorers in big games but more especially the try scorers. As a genuine superstar and someone of unparalleled ability, Jason Robinson may have played in games in which he got more plaudits, made more spectacular breaks and dotted down tries. But as a tactical display of full-back play, and a mental level of courage and intensity, observed by someone who played beside him in the same back-three axis, this game was one of his finest.

We won but on a technical level we weren't playing that well. The defence in particular had taken a step back from the way it had performed on the previous tour. The system England played was in stark contrast to Wasps' blitz. Drilled by the ever-professional Phil Larder, England's was a safer and more reliable system but it was more passive, relying on the cover defence getting from one side of the field to the other. Without moving forward first, with good line speed as we had done on the previous tour and as we managed to get back to by the final stages, it meant that a team could move the ball from side to side, retaining the ball and eventually making ground.

If you watch any tapes of the England team during this period, the majority of scores were made on the outside after multi-phase attacks. Without an individual making a one-on-one mistake, and where there are enough numbers to mark up the opposition, the score will be generated by a lack of line speed from the inside. Without moving up quickly from the inside, it meant that the men further out couldn't move up quickly without leaving the line. Thus you would either have to risk leaving a dog-leg shape in your defensive line, which is easier to attack, or wait for them to go on your outside and use the drift to tackle them next to the touchline but conceding ground.

This system was exploited by Samoa in the opening periods of the next game, on 26 October. Eventually, without moving forward to start with, a defence will run out of steam by the time it has made its umpteenth trek across the park and in that way Samoa, moving the ball from one side to the other, taking a bit of ground each time, scored the first try against the tournament favourites, although we finally beat them 35–22.

I had struggled with a tight calf that week and the medics deemed me unfit to play. The team got a decent rotation and though being neck and neck for long periods, we eventually managed to control the ball long enough for Phil Vickery to cross for the winning score.

We'd won, but after South Africa racked up fifty points against the Samoans there were some anxious looks and a degree of frustration. We knew that we weren't operating on a level that would win us the cup.

The last game of the group, on 2 November, was more a training run, but certainly a much-needed tonic before the storm clouds that were gathering. Uruguay were a team full of part-timers, there not only to do their country proud taking part in the world's premier competition, but also to embrace the aspects of rugby football that professionalism does not often allow time for.

Playing against a less complete side it was an absolute joy to be 'put away' into space or given an early opportunity that, in all honesty, hadn't been created since the French warm-up game at Twickenham. The temptation on such occasions is that everyone gets greedy, people get lazy waiting for the glory pass and stop doing their jobs. Fortunately for the boys out wide, the lads stayed very disciplined for the large part, the forwards doing the hard yards, releasing the ball on the front foot, for the midfield to put the quick boys into space. It was this discipline to stick to your job that led to the impressive score-line and for me, fortunately, as the main strike runner, as full back bagging a world record five tries in our 111–13 victory. Though it sounds obvious, it was enjoyable stuff and the sort of rugby that had made every one of us want to take up the game in the first place.

On a slightly more humorous note, Joe Worsley played on the blind-side flank on that day. A rippling seventeen-stone lump of pure athletic muscle, he misjudged a tackle on the opposing fly half and got sin-binned. Bearing in mind that the player he had pole-axed was a ten-stone amateur with a full-time job outside of rugby playing for the honour and joy of representing his country, Joe somewhat misread the applause that rained down as he walked off the field.

Having garrotted poor Pablo, leaving him twitching on the ground, Joe bowed and clapped to the crowd on his lonesome stroll to the dug-out. In fact, the crowd were giving the Uruguayan fly half an encouraging clap to help him back to his feet again, not applauding the big bully who'd just ruined the party. Joe, being the most amiable and gentle of characters, meant no harm or offence but, not exactly being Clive's favourite person, he got a telling-off and was made to apologise.

Talking of Joe, if you ever get the chance to ask him about his conduct in our team meetings you'll be amused. Sitting next to him, you'd notice him scribbling notes to himself: 'Don't say anything!', 'Don't say anything!', 'Don't say anything!', at which point the pressure would become too great, the dam would burst and he would come out with a technical point drawing the coach's attention to a specific area. That was it! It was like watching a car crash in slow motion – that moment of agony you felt for him knowing what the response would be. No matter what was said, no matter how relevant the point he was making, the coach's response was brutal – a metaphorical, chain-fed, .50-calibre abuse was fired in his direction, leaving him reeling with bemusement and the rest of us cringing at the sight of such merciless destruction. True to form, though, his skin thicker than most, he would come right back again jovially for another belt of fire in the next meeting.

Following the completion of the first group matches, we moved to Brisbane, the base for the quarter-finals. Not a member of the COT, I suspected that there were some tough words being spoken behind the scenes. The team was picked for Wales, our next opponents, but there seemed to be a slight uncertainty as to how we were to play the game. It is a credit to the management structure and team leadership laid down by Johnson and his raft of lieutenants that no uncertainty was visible to the public.

It was this ability and mutual trust that formed the cornerstone of this successful operation. It was a collaboration of minds that worked, but most of all it was the fact that people listened to other's views, taking them on board and shaping the week accordingly. Unfortunately this two-way relationship ceased after the World Cup, but more on that later.

The Uruguay game apart, we had reverted to being a fairly conservative team, winning, but not as convincingly as we had done before the tournament. Tension therefore began to mount and, from a personal point of view, things took a turn for the worse after I slipped on a new pair of Oliver Sweeneys.

Along with Hackett, Oliver Sweeney was the official clothing sponsor, providing the squad with some rather elegant leather shoes. Having been in the rather relaxed environment of Western Australia, being back in a bigger city seemed like the suitable time to don the new pair of chestnut slips. Unfortunately, having not been outside their box, the soles were like polished glass and my right foot slipped on the plush hotel carpet. For anyone who's never pulled a muscle, it feels like a quick electric shock. Though not serious, it just didn't feel quite right and at the back of my mind I hoped that it would be right for the game.

I'd been to the masseuse at the hotel and complained of it being tight and feeling a bit odd, but not exactly injured as such. It wasn't so bad as to stop me training, but being my right hamstring I just wasn't confident enough to put full power through it and sprint. I warmed up thoroughly before the final team run, hoping it would be OK and loosen off, and started the session as usual. The dilemma was huge. Anyone who's played professional sport has faced a similar situation at some stage in their career. Do you risk it, hoping it will be OK? If you pull out will you be picked the following week? If we lost and I hadn't played, could I live with myself thinking, what if? If I played and it was fine, but playing on my mind, would it affect my game? Such questions are the reality of playing top-level sport. Ideally you would never play with an injury, but how bad does it have to be to constitute an injury? Is it just a niggle, or is it just in your head? If it's just pain, you can manage that as most players do week in, week out, taking various painkillers and coaching your mind to switch off from that – safe in the knowledge you're not going to do yourself any harm. But what if you are risking further damage?

So, having given up a career to get involved again in the setup, being now a regular in the team, with five minutes left of the session before the biggest game of my life I decided to pull myself out. My reasoning being that it didn't feel right and, for the sake of the team, a fully fit Dan Luger or Iain Balshaw was better than a nearly fit Josh Lewsey.

My fears as to the repercussions weren't exactly correct. They were three times worse. This was a scenario in which tensions ran high anyway, crossing the borders between the coach's selection, the fitness staff and the entire medical team. Clive was livid with everyone, but especially with me. The main issue was that they'd all seen me doing strides beforehand and would not accept that this was a legitimate warm-up for a tight or niggly hamstring. I'd also apparently put the medical team and fitness team under fire by not reporting the slip as an 'injury' in the first place. Understandably, everyone saw this as a breaking of faith and dishonesty on my part, but playing with injuries all the time, not initially considering it that severe, and having a high-maintenance body anyway, at first it didn't even seem worth mentioning. It wasn't till we got to the session that I realised it was worth bringing up and, in fairness, I had lots of rubs in order to loosen it beforehand.

Clive, as any decision-maker would, liked his injury audit to be in black and white, but the reality is often grey. At such a late stage it's the last thing that's needed, but after making the necessary changes we convened for a meeting back at the hotel.

He'd already called Austin Healey and I was off home! No, this couldn't be. His reasoning was that with a dodgy hamstring I was no use, would take three weeks to recover (the usual period for a grade-one tear), wouldn't be fit for the final stages and thus I had to go for someone who was.

I couldn't believe it, and felt that my world and all I'd worked for was crumbling apart in some crappy conference room in the basement of our hotel. Then Simon Kemp, to his eternal credit and my enormous gratitude, intervened. In his measured and dulcet tones – a welcome change from the irate bluntness of the management and my incredulous pleading – suggested having a scan done first, flying Austin over in case, but putting him on hold till we knew the results and could decide accordingly. This was, to tell the truth, the most sensible solution and off we trotted for the MRI.

I got a certain amount of credit when we got the imaging. Not a full tear, but a slight pool of intramuscular bleeding – supporting the symptoms of it not feeling quite right but still being manageable. The reality was that if I had played it would have gone completely and there'd have been no semis or final for me, so the decision to pull out was at least the correct one. Although the odds still didn't look good for a full recovery in time for the following week I was given till the Wednesday to prove my fitness. A window of opportunity!

So with the consultation of some trusted physios back at home and Phil Pask, the Duracell Bunny team physio, we cracked on with accelerated rehab.

More importantly, the boys played a resurgent Welsh side at the Suncorp Stadium in Brisbane on 9 November. They started well, we looked somewhat bemused and kicked poorly to their counter-attacking strengths. Our attack was poor and disjointed with Wales going in unexpectedly ahead at half-time. Bearing in mind this was the same team that the 'Possibles' had put fifty points on two months before, we were coming off the rails in yet another World Cup quarter-final.

With thirty minutes to go Clive made the call that saved England and possibly kept us in the competition. Mike Catt came on at inside centre, not so much for his dynamic individual play, but to steady the ship, for the length of his kicking and, most importantly, to coax Jonny into making the right calls. The game changed immediately and suddenly England were in front. Helped by a quite remarkable individual run by Jason that was capped by that greatest of try scavengers, Will Greenwood, Jonny found his kicking boots again, Wales succumbed 28–17 and we were through to the semis in Sydney on 16 November.

The dynamics I mentioned before about it being a two-way relationship between the management and COT then really kicked in as the length, duration, intensity and type of training altered massively. Jonny would still need a sleeping bag and poncho for the amount of time he spent out on the training paddock, but the rest of us were limited to twenty-minute walk-throughs.

Having been through months of flogging, we didn't need to do the hard stuff, just making sure we were fresh for kick-off. However, when the body is used to working hard day in, day out, it craves it when it's not made to do so; and thus, with the three meals and two snacks a day laid on, with little else to break the monotony, it was a challenge not to spend all day grazing. If you look at the size and weight of our players by the time we reached the final, I can't imagine there have been many heavier teams in rugby history.

Austin was now in and around the hotel although technically not being allowed to do so under competition rules; he'd come to the lobby for the lads to abuse him. He was never one to shy away from the banter, and I did actually feel terribly sorry for him when he was eventually sent home again without being included. Every day Clive would jokingly ask me if he could send him home yet. D-day came on the Wednesday when we walked to the nearby cricket ground in Manly in which Pasky and I had done our rehab each day since arriving in Sydney. By this stage, rugby euphoria had gripped the travelling British fans and getting out of the hotel without the paparazzi engulfing and following us was difficult enough. Luckily we used one of the fire exits and walked to the empty training ground just around the corner. I say empty; it was, all except one person – Clive. Feeling confident and jovial I thought it'd be funny to pretend to twinge the hamstring on my second run through before carrying on as usual. It went down like a bacon sandwich at a bar mitzvah, so needless to say I kept my head down for the rest of the reps!

Though it may burn Kieran, Daws and other good mates of his, as abuse sits far more easily than praise, I have always considered Austin Healey to be one of the best and most complete rugby players never to reach greatness. Despite his Leicester lip, he was always an immensely intelligent player blending the rare ability of athleticism and footballing ability with drive and competitiveness. I believe that if he'd settled on his more natural position earlier in his rugby career, perhaps he would have been in the squad from the start.

The boys were ruthless in their cruelty: 'chin up Aus, you've picked up plenty of air miles . . .' It was good-humoured stuff and he played along, but deep down you knew it must have been painful for him not to be part of things. I didn't say a word.

Catt was in for Tindall, I was back to full back and the Telstra Stadium was like the Albert Hall. 'Rule, Britannia!', 'Jerusalem', 'Land of Hope and Glory' – all were belted out by the tens of thousands of English fans both inside and outside the ground. With such historical significance, England–France games are always special. The tabloids only need a glimpse of the cockerel and the blue shirt for Waterloo and Agincourt to be rolled out, but this was the semi-final of the rugby World Cup, so national pride, yes, but xenophobic racism? Not a chance.

We played well in difficult conditions. Jonny had his best game of the tournament, being both tactically astute and, with Daws, varying play brilliantly. Despite France scoring first, we played an excellent pressure game, keeping the ball for long periods and keeping the scoreboard ticking whenever we got in their third. Without droning on for too long, the game is best summed up by one quote in particular which came out of the 2007 World Cup. The French had long been critics of the English game, lambasting it for its lack of flair. This was wet weather, we'd beaten every major team in the world with an all-court game, and who remembers the team that loses in the semis anyway (on this occasion France, by 27 points to 7)? Thomas Castaigne said in the studio before the 2007 semi to Martin Johnson:

TC: In Australia, you never looked like scoring [a try].
MJ: Yeah, that's probably true . . . but you never looked like winning!

The hamstring held out, the trials and tribulations of the previous week had all been worthwhile, and we were in the World Cup final! Pinch yourself time . . .

Chapter 12

The Final

'JUST TREAT IT like any normal game . . .'

Well, it's not really, is it? Driving around on the Saturday morning to your mates' houses, persuading them to get their arses out of bed and leave their other halves for a few hours to roll around in the mud and stopping on the way for a pre-match Big Mac isn't quite the same as a global audience of one billion people!

It was a bizarre week and in the run-up to any major competition the best you can do is to try to live a normal existence. As mentioned, our hotel on Manly Beach was now surrounded by a thousand fans day and night, happy for the slightest chance of seeing/cheering the boys, but especially Johnno, Golden Balls or Sir Clive, as he was now affectionately known amongst them.

On a personal note, I tried to embrace the mentality that had served me so well since my return from the wilderness and had delivered for me earlier in the year – that is, to know my own mind, stay away from the noise and fuss, keep a level head and try to convince myself that I wasn't bothered what the coaches around me thought of my game, since I was my harshest critic anyway. This was a game to 'front up', no matter what else was going on.

In big finals and other tight games, back-three players can, on occasion, have limited impact and involvement. Obviously I'd want to be involved all the time, carrying ball, making tackles and running in tries, but the reality of cup final football isn't like that. Selfishly, if you judge yourself by how well you've played, quite often in the biggest games the back-three players will walk off delighted that their team has won, but feeling somewhat empty or unfulfilled, knowing that they would have liked to contribute more. The point is that at this stage of competition it isn't about giving everyone a go, or making everyone feel good about their performance; it's about winning, pure and simple. To that end the game very rarely opens up as the boys out wide would sometimes like, but it is more a case of play in their half and take points whenever they're on offer. That explains how and why Wasps have peaked so well technically and performed consistently on the final stage and why, as I mentioned earlier, we ended up having such a convincing score-line against Ireland in the Grand Slam decider and eventually against France in the semi.

The other aspect of mental preparation is a very significant but also an incredibly individual one. Everyone is different. Vicks, being the most laid-back individual off the field, likes a nice, calculated build-up; Lawrence, by his own admission, likes (and I quote) to come out 'bared-up and steaming'; Will is always on hand to crack jokes and keeps a somewhat objective view; and old Jonny boy is always left to do his thing, safe in the knowledge that if he does his stuff we'll all be happy afterwards.

Watching television while typing this up, there was a programme about the Commando Brigade's raid on St Nazaire in the Second World War. As my brother-in-law is currently fighting a bloody and dirty conflict in Helmand with 2 Para, which puts things into a more personal and immediate perspective, a quote from one of the survivors of 1942 rang particularly true: 'The definition of courage is to identify your fear and conquer it.'

For these heroes it meant operating and performing their tasks under conditions of appalling danger, when the natural human instinct is to keep your head down and hide. For us, though it's far less significant and always a little bit embarrassing to compare sport with a serious subject like battle, it's all relative – fears still exist and need conquering all the same so that you can perform and ultimately succeed. It is the fear of failure, but what does that mean? For me personally, I don't fear losing – that's just sport and if you're beaten by a better team or opponent, there isn't much more you can say about it. However, what I do fear is not performing, not playing to my potential or, in this case, and worse still, making the mistake that could lose your country the World Cup.

We knew that whatever happened on the day would live with us for the rest of our lives, either filling us with joy and pride or remaining to haunt or torture us. In an earlier paragraph I wrote of my personal need to 'front up' in the forthcoming final. Some people – and I know Shaun Edwards is among them – would say I was thinking too much, but firstly there is not much else to do when you're cocooned in a hotel, and secondly it is important to understand and channel your fears. Personally I take solace from the knowledge that if I can walk off the field after a game, look at myself in the mirror and know I've given everything, that I've not been hindered or inhibited by the fear of making a mistake, then I can live with myself. That to me is the definition of 'fronting up'.

The excuse that if we lost it would be to the better team wasn't really acceptable. We *knew* deep down that we were the better side and had beaten Australia on the three previous occasions to prove it. Frankly we didn't want to be using excuses either; that wasn't part of this team's culture or character. You can always find excuses, and to search them out before the event is somewhat defeatist anyway. We needed to be coming home with the cup – end of story.

If all this seems a little too theoretical and philosophical, it works if you see it as a snapshot of the thoughts and anxieties that swirl around in your head in the build-up to such a game, when you have too much time to think. Consequently, I did what I'd do at home with a big game looming: go and see my mates.

'Bastards! Can't you lot shut up and talk about something except bloody rugby? I'm trying to switch off here!'

Failing that, and to the management's disgust, I'd sneak off surfing . . .

Sydney was quite a special place to be at the time. We were somewhat hemmed in by the swathes of rugby fans turning the entire city centre into a booze-fuelled party. Australia is genuinely a brilliantly vibrant place in its own right, but with the added dimension of hosting a major sporting event, with its home team in the final against the 'motherland', there can be few better places to be. It is almost a shame that being involved with the game itself you didn't really get the chance to enjoy the whole atmosphere, as my mates certainly were. And as part of your preparation, it was always amusing to have your university pals texting in the early hours, drunk messages of affection with the odd bit of tactical advice thrown in. Funnily enough, I didn't pass on the ones that started 'Tell Johnno . . .' or 'Tell Clive . . .'

The papers at home and in Oz were, of course, full of rugby articles: about who thought what, how the teams were shaping up and, by this stage, inevitably, the girly gossip stuff – 'who's fittest?', 'who's single?' and 'what about the other halves?' I'd say that 80 per cent of the lads had stopped reading the press by now, trying in their own ways to switch off from the huge attention that rugby was getting and attempting in some small way to remain level-headed and normal in this pressure-cooker environment.

With my pals in Sydney understandably rather engrossed in the pre-match build-up and not being much use before 11 a.m. and outside necking Yager bombs and Snakey B, I kept in contact with some of my army pals who, fighting the second Gulf War, had enough going on in their own lives to keep their feet firmly planted on the ground. Ed Cleland, who eventually went into my regiment of choice, 7 Para Royal Horse Artillery, was now a troop commander, doing as I would have been doing, firing a battery of light gun as part of the rapid-reaction 16 Air Assault Brigade. Their having to 'stand to' in the desert at first and last light each day with the fear of NBC (nuclear, biological and chemical) warfare heading their way certainly forced me to put my own nerves into perspective.

Paul Adams, my old 'civilian chum' and the biggest drill pig in Sandhurst's three-hundred-year history, was also fighting some horrendous face-to-face battles with Ba'th Party representatives. Talking to him on his return offered, in my experience, some of the most revealing and explicit insights into the ugliness, complexity and reality of modern counter-insurgency warfare. As was to be expected, Paul handled himself and his men in exemplary fashion, winning plaudits and the approval of his superiors on his return, which in typical style he ignored, following his own path as he saw best.

My former army colleagues Marcus Milne-Home, Rob Honan, Dan Hinxman, Adam Roberts and others were all on the sort of operations that made playing a game for eighty minutes (or a hundred, as it turned out) pale into insignificance by comparison and again helped me not to get too wound up.

Martin Johnson made a point at the start of the week that was particularly relevant. Rugby players are not used to the celebrity lifestyle, most preferring the shadows of anonymity. This, as the game becomes increasingly professional, is changing and will continue to do so. At that stage, football did not dominate as it now does, and consequently the commercial opportunities available in rugby were both novel and, to the uninitiated, mind-bogglingly rewarding.

Agents were busy lining up countless endorsement contracts, and the offer of huge cash-in-hand payments just to show up at an event that week for five minutes meant that, for some, you could have doubled your entire World Cup earnings.

Martin's words were prescient. 'Lads, everyone will be after your time at the moment – agents, contacts, friends and even families. You've got the rest of your lives to do all that stuff. Just for one more week, don't do anything. We've come so far, don't f**k it up now, let's just win this thing first, then you can do what you want.'

Absolutely spot on! So that was it; everyone got blanked. The only person who had separate issues was Steve Thompson who planned on proposing to his girlfriend on the beach the morning after the final. Wally was always a good pal of mine and I used to enjoy popping into his room to hear his alter ego deliberating over what he was going to say to her.

So the week went by, the lads living in a goldfish bowl, gorging on the endless meals and spending an unhealthy amount of time watching the female beach volleyball championships take place in front of the hotel.

Friday night and, after the team meeting, another high-carb meal of lasagne, Thai green chicken curry and pudding. Then, feeling like Roland from *Grange Hill*, we all departed for the last night's sleep before the World Cup final. Simon Kemp always keeps a decent supply of Zoplicane (sleeping tablets), and knowing what was at stake the following night, the boys were swallowing them like sweets.

On final day, bearing in mind that you're not kicking off till 8 p.m, you try and go back to bed. Not a chance. At school and minis we used to play at 10.30 in the morning, so after some snap and putting your kit on, there was little chance for anything else. Twelve hours of tossing and turning, visualising and trying to ignore what was going on: I could now see why Mike Tindall and Iain Balshaw were complete ninjas on every computer game.

Game time at last and the ground was pumping. Like some sort of state-run propaganda exercise, the Aussies had amusingly bathed the Sydney Opera House, the Harbour Bridge and great swathes of the stadium crowd in gold lighting. I've no idea who comprised the bulk of the crowd that night, but knowing the price of the tickets (as players we got two free and the rest were £400 each) and the frequency with which Australia won medals in comparison to us, I'm guessing the majority were English.

All summer long we'd trained for hot-weather football. Dave Reddin had asked Powerade to design a special high-phosphate low-sugar hydration drink, and Nike and the rest of the sportswear companies had designed special cleats and moulded studs to be comfortable yet grip on the hard turf. The reality for the closing stages was rain, 18 mil sprigs (studs for the wet conditions) and the going most definitely soft.

I don't remember much of the game in all honesty; you tend not to in such highly charged atmospheres. Our defence was monumental throughout, the intensity of the hits relentless and, knowing our aggressive line speed, Steve Larkham, an all-time great 10 in my book, accurately kicked high and wide behind our line for the tall and athletic Lote Tuqiri to outjump the comparative Oompa-Loompas in Jason and myself. After that, we controlled the game, but the impressive and downright courageous kicking of Elton Flatley, along with some oft-referred-to decisions by referee Andre Watson at scrums, kept Australia within touch. A well-known story that most within the rugby fraternity have heard is that, having met the front-row lads in the week before the final, in which it was widely regarded we had the edge, Mr Watson stated that he wouldn't give a scrum penalty unless he was prepared to put his mortgage on it.

So after the fourth scrum penalty against us, which our boys felt was a little unjustified, Steve Thompson came out with the quote of the day:

'Andre, about that mortgage . . . You must have a shit house!'

Tins, back in the team for his horsepower and ability to stop the ever-impressive Mortlock in his tracks, also kicked brilliantly that day, one of which gave me a one-on-one against the bigger man. I fancied myself in a straight foot race and was enraged when Watson failed to give a penalty for blatant obstruction when he cut me up just as I was pulling past. With Tuqiri having to turn and fall, I wanted to smash him in response and, fair dos, he did me like a kipper. Seeing me flying he dummied to rise and sent me somersaulting over the top, missing the tackle. After that I gathered my thoughts and got my head back on to the game, trying to ball carry wherever possible.

Within a few minutes, the team were back up the Australian end and I had a one-on-one with George Gregan three yards out. That quick thought of 'take him on' does flash through your mind at such moments, but though I thought I could probably make it, we had a three-on-two outside and thus I slipped the ball to Daws and he on to Ben Kay to go in untouched . . . but no, he drops it! What people don't know, and in fairness to Ben, ninety-nine times out of a hundred he would take that pass, but that night he was wearing some of those wet-weather gloves for the first time ever, which thankfully he discarded soon afterwards and, to his credit, regained his focus and, after the match, was able to laugh about it. A lesser soul would have crumpled at such a point.

Another thing that people forget is that Jonny missed four drop goals in that final. These four were on his favoured left foot, so it was doing the rounds afterwards that someone had said 'give the other one a go'. Personally I think he was just playing the crowd, as we all know he's the heavy-drinking, druggy, gambling type!

The rest, as they say, is history, but it did feel throughout, from the first to the last, that our side was due a win. It's difficult to explain this; there was just a feeling of inevitability about it, nothing arrogant, but sometimes in an individual's and team's evolution there comes a moment of destiny. The game had lasted a hundred minutes, and had produced a quite staggering dramatic sporting event, whether you were a rugby fan or not. Sport has the ability to cross boundaries, build relationships and lift an entire nation. England rose.

Back at home the whole country partied in pubs and bars, strangers embraced, as we were now, for the first time for thirty-seven years in a major sport, the World Champions!

People asked afterwards, 'Has it sunk in?' For most the answer was 'Not yet'. It's the quiet moments of reflection that allow our private selves to be exposed, but for me it was instantaneous, when I saw my family in the crowd.

A lot of people sacrifice an awful lot for you to be able to put rugby first. Your friends, family and loved ones help you through all of life's struggles, whether they drove you around the country, washed your kit, or nursed your wounds. As friends, they're there to pick up the pieces when you doubt yourself, sharing the good times and the bad. You miss out on weddings, stag dos, christenings, nights on the lash, birthdays, just spending time together, so that you can prepare for the next game or train effectively, time that you can't get back, and sometimes you ask yourself if you're doing the right thing.

I had my entire family there, and though the following sentiments will cause some embarrassment, I'm not ashamed to say that, despite having a very fortunate and privileged upbringing, it wasn't entirely without pain. I was, according to my family, a very difficult child and, needless to say, as with so many other families, there were some difficult issues which they'd say were either caused by me or I was in some way connected to. If you have a great game so do they; if you win so do they. My friends laugh at the alpha-maleness of our clan as we've never been ones to touch, cuddle or even, on most occasions, talk, but in one look I got all I'd ever needed.

Every weight I'd ever lifted, every sprint session on my own in the field, every blow-out when your mates were partying, every injury and sacrifice and choice I'd ever had to take, every fight, argument and pain suffered had all been made worth it by that look. My life had been worth it. Someone was proud of me.

There are times in our life when we wish we'd acted differently, others when we wish we hadn't let the moment pass without doing or saying something. I was an open book and couldn't contain my emotion.

Clive rather poignantly put his arm around me as we walked back to the dressing room. This man whose thoughts and opinions had tortured and consumed my conscience, this man who had plagued my actions and seemed to mistrust me for so long was now embracing me as one of his own in his greatest of moments.

I walked back down the tunnel ahead of Johnson and Dallaglio, safe in the knowledge that I could die happy.

Chapter 13

Party

AMONG THE MANY CHORES involved in playing international rugby are the post-match obligations. When given the chance to enjoy yourself, or let your hair down, the functions can be quite fun, although the majority of the time you're rushing straight back afterwards to prepare for the next game, so these occasions become an unwanted extra. The other formality is the press room, or 'walking the line'. The press guys are for the most part reasonably fair and bright individuals and know full well what they're going to write or how they saw the game. Why, then, has it always been mandatory for players to be available after every game? 'What do you want to know . . . I was rubbish?', or 'Wasn't I brilliant?' By and large it seems to offer an unwarranted opportunity for you to slip up after a highly charged game and to blurt out something you'll later regret. I was taught to be honest and truthful but that can often be misconstrued as being too forthright or cocky. The end result is that you become increasingly conscious about not upsetting anyone. If you challenge your superiors in coaching/management and the hierarchy with an informed opinion that somehow crosses the 'party line', it is seen as dishonourable and disloyal.

It's understandable, then, that young players, or even those that do not want to run the risk of making enemies and getting dropped, spout nothing but pointless rhetoric.

On such occasions, most players time their run through the press room, waiting at the entrance for a try scorer, a captain or a Jonny so that as they wander in and get pounced on you can exit stage right unscathed and untouched. The World Cup final was a different matter. Those who've studied GCSE history, grown up in Kim Jong-Il's North Korea or voted in 'democratic' Zimbabwe will understand something of the word propaganda. Touring Australia as an England team is no different. Although it's slightly more jovial, and with more fun and banter, especially compared to New Zealand, it is sometimes astonishing what is written about people who have given absolutely no fuel or evidence to support such stories.

After the final – when the whole of Christendom seemed to be partying, and, having spent months hidden away, living as pariahs, we couldn't wait to get out and join them – we had to 'do the press' for half an hour first. For the entire time we'd been in Australia, toeing the party line, saying all the right things and taking the flak, we had no credit or respect from the Australian media for the humility we had shown. But now, having just achieved the ultimate, the gloves were discarded and the boys just let rip. Having received their winners' medals from a particularly ungracious John Howard, it was amusing to see some of our bigger lads, brows furrowed, fingers pointing, towering over the same Aussie press that had been lambasting us for months. It was sweet justice and I've kept a copy of the *Sydney Morning Herald* that I was given at 0600 hours in the Cargo nightclub as a reminder of the respect that we'd at last won.

Understandably the lads were in a fairly intolerant mood. They also dismissed (the then minister for sport) Tessa Jowell's attempt to enter the dressing room.

So, with the ever popular Princes William and Harry in tow, everyone finally went out to meet the families and friends to start the celebrations.

The various stories of the ensuing piss-ups will live on for many a year in rugby folklore. Some are already well known on the rugby dinner circuit and, frankly, are a lot funnier told by people other than me, but it isn't every day you become a world champion.

On a more personal note, I got in after the first night at about 11 a.m., but bearing in mind we didn't get out till gone two in the morning it wasn't anything unusual. After a quick photo on the beach and a word from Clive, we left straight away for the IRB awards dinner. We went straight through the following night again, planning to get on the plane on the Monday morning. Bearing in mind that we hadn't really been to bed since Friday night I was now officially in 'clip' and couldn't wait for the BA Club World flat beds on the way home. So just as soon as we got on board, I snuggled up with my blanket, ear-plugs and mask, only for my worst fears to be realised.

'Hello, son!'

Shocker!

They'd only gone and allocated the seats alphabetically ... Luger, Lewsey, LEONARD!

'You'll 'ave a drink with Uncle Jase?'

I was in rags, looked like death. For goodness' sake, we were supposed to be meeting the Queen on Wednesday! So after even more booze and while he wasn't looking, having saved up some surplus Zoplicane from Simon over the course of the trip I methodically dropped sleeping tablets into his wine.

One is a strong human dose. It took three to tranquilise him! He finally fell asleep with a bread roll in his mouth somewhere over the desert.

* * *

The whole period following that memorable night in Sydney was one that just didn't feel quite real. Although we played the following weekend, the lads were getting invitations to this, that and the other. For the first time in our country's history, rugby players were now 'celebrities'. Although I personally never felt a part of that whole thing, it very quickly became apparent that some did and courted the possibilities that the bright lights had to offer.

The only member of the squad single at the time was Mike Tindall, and so the gossip columns had a field day with him, trying to expose this situation and open doors on to that. It was around about that time that he began dating Zara Phillips, the enormously grounded and amiable Royal with more than enough drive to succeed in her own right. It seemed straight away to be a well-suited match and although I'm still waiting for the stories about the family Christmas, I'm sure it's no coincidence that soon afterwards, with Mike's composed influence, Zara became a world champion in her own sport.

Collectively, eyes were now opened to the commercial, corporate and media opportunities that follow from a success such as winning the World Cup. Though it is easy to be judgemental, most players' forms dipped after they came home. This is perhaps understandable, but, under the leadership of Warren and Shaun, the Wasps boys were actively encouraged to go and celebrate, but in return they demanded a 'front up at game time' mentality that maintained all our hunger for success.

One commercial opportunity that did come our way was in the shape of celebrity magazines. Not understanding that industry, having little knowledge of it and with the vast majority of rugby agents at the time being quite low-level negotiators rather than PR-savvy strategists, it was a case of grab it while you can. *Hello!* magazine approached most of the players and offered to take a few pictures. My initial thoughts were, no way, but after they'd doubled their offer, promising to be in the house for three hours max – nothing controversial, just cheesy shots – and, more importantly, seven others from the team, more experienced than me, were doing it too, I thought, sod it, why not? It was pretty amazing money for something that wasn't doing any harm and I worked out how many broken noses playing rugby I'd have to get to earn the equivalent.

What you didn't realise was that in letting the media in you were effectively agreeing to open season on your private life. That was fine if you were a settled, married man with kids, but as someone who soon afterwards split up with his girlfriend, it was a real eye-opener.

The guys could, if they organised themselves well, legitimately earn as much outside the game as they could from just playing it.

Wasps were flying; we were the best team in Europe, playing brilliant, challenging rugby in a fun but dynamic environment. Being back at the club, the familiarity of your own bed was more than welcome. Though it would have been possible to spend every night of the week on the fun and lively charity dinner and testimonial circuit, a night at home with the dogs was far more pleasurable. The high life had to be lived for a while as it was novel, fun and exciting, but soon it started to take its toll and you'd begin to crave life's simpler pleasures. The ramifications of winning the cup still go on today, with a never-ending list of invites, but at some point you have to get a grip on your own life and stop living in the past.

Lawrence Dallaglio and I were the only Wasps actually to play in the final but the rest of our contingent were also keen to impress their new world champions status on the domestic scene. Simon Shaw had always performed week in, week out, but since that time, for me, in particular has emerged as the most significant forward in English rugby.

Wasps won the double that year, season 2003–4, and, though I'm biased, in my opinion we played in one of the greatest games professional rugby history has yet seen. To get there we played and beat Perpignan home and away, at their Stade Aimé Giral. The game was more akin to bare-knuckle fighting than rugby, with the medics getting through three times the number of sutures than normal, but in order to win the Heineken Cup, amongst other things, you have to prove at some point that you're the best team. We beat Perpignan twice in the group (28–7 and 34–6), followed by Gloucester in the quarters (34–3), Munster in the semis (37–32) and Toulouse (27–20) – Europe's largest club – in the final. Toulouse, according to Will Greenwood, played the best rugby that a losing team had ever played, which again speaks volumes for our defence and our resolve, but the game that stood out for me was Munster in the semis. That year the Heineken Cup really came of age and for the first time started producing rugby of a higher quality and intensity than international test matches.

There are some days that are just advertisements for their sport. In comparison you can come up with Ali/Foreman (1974), Federer/Nadal (2008), Michael Johnson (1996), Shane Warne/England (on numerous occasions), but as far as rugby goes the semi-final was an epic. The crowd at Lansdowne Road's last game consisted of 48,500 singing Munster fans dressed in red. That left about 1,500 Wasps. The game changed hands six times, it was won in the dying seconds and the atmosphere was as generous and as sporting as you'll find anywhere. When cynical rugby hacks describe it as a game to go down in history, you know it's been fairly special.

All in all, 2003–4 had been a vintage year. Lifting the World Cup, building family bridges, doing the domestic and European double and dipping into an alien but increasingly lucrative commercial world, it had been one to savour, but unfortunately the fortunes of the national team had begun to dip and, with the weight of expectation, questions were beginning to be asked.

Chapter 14

Leadership

I T IS A LITTLE-KNOWN fact that I've played more games for England since the 2003 World Cup than anyone else. Although there have been periods when I've been left out of the international team, it is not something I dwell on; that smacks of under-achievement, the acceptance of mediocrity and justification through excuses.

Wasps on the other hand, have, with limited resources, for the large part continued to be the hub of challenging, successful dynamism, becoming the most successful team in professional rugby history. But why has this been the case? What is it that makes a team successful or otherwise? Why, since 2003, with the exception of a smattering of one-off performances and two quality results when it mattered most during the 2007 World Cup, has the national team fallen from the lofty heights it reached in those halcyon days?

Ask various coaches and they will say players; players point to coaches, and managers point to resources. The real answer is probably a combination of factors. In order to get the definitive answer you would need the analytical skills that every rugby body in the world craves – some people have better skills than others and they are the successful ones. It's time for me to climb on to my metaphorical soapbox again. To my mind you need to understand the components that make up a professional sporting environment.

There are four basic but different components of a rugby team (and possibly of any sporting side, but I have no experience of others so I can't comment):

LEADERSHIP: the elements of strategy, vision, decision-making and rank structure.

MANAGEMENT: the man management and handling of inter-relationships.

COACHING: the technical element of how a team and the individuals within it are to play.

PLAYERS: those who take the field.

Inevitably there is some overlapping, as can be seen in the following diagram, but these are fundamentally different components that to my mind determine whether a team is successful or not.

Leadership first. This is a word that is bandied about regularly, often without a true understanding of what it entails. Any study of leadership will clearly demonstrate that it is not something that comes in a single, specific form. Leaders can be dictators, democrats, passive, cajoling types, tyrants or bullies; sometimes these are effective, sometimes not. There are certain predominant character traits that make for good leaders, but the style of leadership needs to suit the particular situation since different styles may work better in different circumstances. A historical example of this is Winston Churchill. His belligerence was exactly what was needed during the war but it was deemed unsuitable once peace had been achieved. In English sport, Brian Clough,

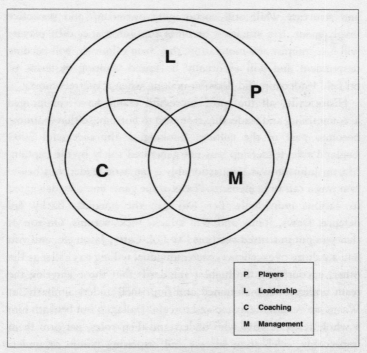

Kevin Bowring, currently Head of Elite Coach Development at the RFU, suggested demonstrating the overlapping and yet different aspects of leadership, management and coaching as shown above

Alex Ferguson and Clive Woodward have all been regarded as great leaders. Clough allegedly once said, 'We'll agree to discuss it, then we'll agree with what I think' – an example of his benign dictatorship. Sources close to Ferguson suggest a similarly tight grip on proceedings and Clive too was definitely the boss of our organisation. The style is irrelevant, of course, if you get the results, and these three certainly did. You don't need to be popular to be successful or, indeed, respected.

With regard to how this relates to players, there is a delicate balance between maintaining authority, installing a vision, strategy and structure while still encouraging ownership and proactive involvement. If a situation becomes too autocratic, then players will lose interest and motivation, they won't flourish, will become despondent and will eventually be found wanting in terms of on-field leadership and decision-making when it matters most.

Historically, all the most successful teams have encouraged accountability and leadership from top to bottom, so that it almost becomes part of the culture. Looking at the successful 2003 England side, leadership was not generated solely by the captain. Martin Johnson was unquestionably a fantastic leader, but below him was a raft of lieutenants. Areas of the game could be delegated to various individuals. Ben Kay ran the lineouts, Backy did defence, Daws, Jonny and Will attack, Vicks scrums. On top of that you put in trusted veterans like Lol, Catty, Jason etc. and you had a culture of excellence, each individual willing to challenge the other, encouraging the highest standards that those entering the team understood, maintained and flourished under. Similarly, at Wasps we've had the iconic and forceful Dallaglio but beneath him a whole team of guys who understand their roles, perform them impeccably, celebrating success and criticising failure or under-achievement wherever it exists. In doing so, the Haskells, Reeses, Skivingtons, Waldoucks and Ciprianis have now evolved into the next generation of Shaws, Kings, Waters and Dallaglios. The challenge isn't, however, just between players; the coaches and managers are also required to pull their weight and to be open and responsive to suggestions from players and each other.

Such a culture is coveted by every coach or manager in sport, but in order to achieve it there has to be a healthy and trusting two-way relationship within the leadership. The best teams are unquestionably player-led, but for this to be achieved the coaches, managers and head honchos have to let it happen, welcoming feedback from players in an environment in which challenging ideas in the right way is seen as positive and constructive rather than disruptive. This will evolve naturally over time in most teams, and that is why successful sides have tended to be more mature and settled with a self-selecting core of senior players. They are a trusted band, which together holds its own power and authority but, ideally, will work in unison with the coaches. But what if you don't have the luxury of time, or, more specifically, if there is no consistency in selection as your decision-making axis (players at 9, 10 and 12) changes each week? Bearing in mind that the players' first objective is to get into the team, will they feel confident enough to challenge the coach's thoughts and thus risk making enemies or being seen as negative and unhappy with the way in which the team is playing? Equally important, will the coach provide an environment that encourages and welcomes feedback? During the transitional period in a team's evolution, or when there is inconsistency in selection, without a successful pattern that the players entirely agree with, it is the hierarchy of leadership that is tested most of all. On the 2005 Lions tour, to hear one of the coaches saying, three days before the first test, that this was 'his session' struck me as being intrinsically wrong.

That said, players are not always right and sometimes need putting back into their boxes too. Ideally, respect for the coach's decisions should be given where it is due. The best coach I've ever had the privilege of working with is Shaun Edwards, but even he hasn't always got the balance quite right. Put simply, he cares so much about the game, how it's played and that his team is successful that he sometimes finds it difficult to sit back, loosen the reins and give those below him their heads. It is no coincidence that our worst season at the club (2005–6) also coincided with Shaun, by his own admission, over-coaching at times. That said, I believe the balance he struck in season 2007–8, when he had the extra stimulation of coaching Wales, was absolutely impeccable. By this stage, with the experienced Ian McGeechan, the intelligent Leon Holden and the analytical Adam Grange, along with Shaun, the entire management team had finally settled into a successful dynamic, knowing how best to manage, interact and bounce ideas off each other. Knowing when to crack the whip, be authoritative and call the shots, or when to step back and encourage others to make their influence felt, is the key to having and indeed generating good leadership.

Leadership, then, obviously has direct crossovers with management, the second important component of a successful rugby team. Making those around you or, especially, below you feel valued, involved and stimulated is more to do with the interpersonal relations and dynamics of management than leadership per se, but putting the structure in place, pulling the strings of control and influence, installing the vision of where the organisation is going and enforcing the strategy so that all that occurs is still part of leadership. You don't necessarily have to be a great manager to be a great leader. Clive was, it is fair to say, a bright man and in my opinion a great leader. He was aware of his shortcomings and appointed technical coaches where he saw that he had limitations. It is also true to say that, immediate post-World Cup apart, he wasn't exactly the cuddly type either, being ruthless when he had to be.

Ian McGeechan is a good manager; he is a kind, loyal, honest and genuine man with the game of rugby's, and each one of his players', interests at heart. That is a skill in itself and, apart from his human qualities, he has the ability to identify individuals' strengths and encourage them to use them. That's not to say he hasn't got a ruthless streak, as he demonstrated last year when he dropped me for the Heineken semi, and Lawrence and other senior players at various times during the season. Far from being an authoritarian, he chooses players and coaches to complement his strengths, just as Clive did; it was under his management that a certain Martin Johnson became captain of the successful 1997 Lions.

Next, coaching. Again there are obvious overlaps with management. You can't be a truly respected leader or manager unless you have an intrinsic knowledge of the game and the players respect that you understand the game as well as they do. Everyone likes to consider himself first and foremost a coach. It is probably the most rewarding and enjoyable part of the job. John Wells, former captain and coach of Leicester and currently forwards coach with England, still joins in the mauling sessions (and don't even ask about his response when someone shouts, 'You'll never take the back seat, will you?'!) Coaching is the closest thing to playing, and anyone who has made it to the management side, to directing operations, will first have donned a tracksuit and imparted his knowledge as a member of the coaching staff.

Most people believe that I had a falling-out with Brian Ashton when he excluded me from the 2008 Six Nations. As far as I am concerned that wasn't the case and I'm certainly not going to write a back-stabbing account of the 2007 World Cup or bitter reflections on a most amiable man. Though we all have our weaknesses, we have our strengths too; Brian's main strength was his coaching. He was – and still is – somewhat revolutionary as a challenging, attacking coach. He encourages his players to think laterally, to enjoy freedom of thought and creation, and discourages a conservative, safety-first approach. He championed the two flat receivers and width approach that served Bath so well in the eighties, took England through their transitional period to becoming the world's best team in the early 2000s and supported countless youngsters who've graduated from his successful National Academy system. During a period of dull and unsuccessful attritional rugby in the eighties he was a coach who dared to be different, chanced his arm and consequently won many domestic trophies. The key to good coaching is the specific technical detail that you pass on to the players. How exactly do you want the team to play, what pattern or structure are they to have as their basic shape, and what have they got to do in order to create the opportunities to score?

Back in the day, coaching was usually done by a single coach, maybe two at a push – one for forwards, another for backs. Now, in the professional game, there is a plethora of coaches – scrummaging, lineouts, attack, defence, fitness, eyesight, kicking, skills and handling, plus a host of others I can't even remember, are all now possible. The two most relevant to what a team does on the field, however, are attack and defence – basically what it does with the ball and what it does without it. There are, of course, periods in the game when no one has the ball and it has to be won in the first place, as well as equally important kick-offs and set pieces, but, leaving such specifics to one side, it's just attack and defence.

With a fit, motivated and intelligent group of players, it is far easier to coach a fairly decent defence than it is an attack. Defence by its very nature is a destructive beast, whereas attack is constructive – it's easier to knock down a house than build it, but that is where the pleasure and thus enjoyment in the game lies. Statistics do show, however, that defence is more important than attack. By and large, each team that has so far won the World Cup has conceded the least number of tries. This also seems to be the case in soccer, rugby league and American football. Wasps deploy a far higher risk form of defence, which, over the course of a season, will never win the mathematics prize at the end-of-season dinner (because statistically it lets through more tries), but in big games, with everyone pumped, it has proved time and time again to be the deciding factor even when we haven't had the ball.

'Attack sells tickets, defence wins championships' – and it's true.

Although you need players to use their own judgement, decision-making and other skills to interact and perform on the field, without a basic structure, framework or pattern they will end up playing as fifteen talented individuals rather than as a cohesive and well-orchestrated unit with a common purpose. This is where good coaching comes in. What happens if he comes this way? What would you like to see me do? How do you want me to play? An example: as a winger for England you were repeatedly told to 'hold your width' – that is, to maintain the team's width of attack, waiting out on the wing for the scoring pass or at least one that would give you the opportunity to score. That's fine if the guys inside are producing the goods and able to work you into space, but if the ball isn't coming and never looks like doing so, at what point do you go off-script and go hunting for it? Wasps, on the other hand, have long encouraged the wingers to be the top ball carriers – which sometimes means more than twenty times a game. That's great for personal involvement, but what if in doing the hard yards you're left with a prop to finish off the scores and he doesn't have the legs to do it as you would have? Again, as with the other aspects, the interaction between coach and players is one of balance and decision-making both on and off the field, with natural crossovers with management and leadership, but the specifics of good, clear and concise coaching are absolutely vital to a team's success. In the best teams I've played in, where everyone had different strengths and abilities, everyone knew their role, what was technically expected of them and how to fit that into the team jigsaw. In the worst teams there was little direction, a lack of cohesion and effectively each individual player was left to ad lib, wasting huge amounts of energy and making it a lottery as to whether or not they had a good game. Playing in such an environment tends to promote selfishness and lack of accountability, because players do not have the pattern of play or the proper springboard that the more successful teams have.

Technical direction doesn't always have to come from the coach; in fact, the team's main decision-makers – 9, 10 and 12 – have the most important roles on the field, providing directions for and demanding responses from those around them. Therefore in the best setups, these players will devise and create with the coaches a pattern of play that everyone feels is workable and progressive. This brings us to the most important part of a team, those at the heart of any side and the ones who take the field – the players.

When all is said and done, good players can still win you games. Conversely, even with the best leadership, management and coaching, if your herd hasn't the pedigree of the one next door, there are only so many rosettes you'll take home. This judging of players rather than the overall setup of the team and how it works as a whole (i.e., in terms of tactics, culture, management and so on) is the area that amuses me most; it's the one that the press are most fickle about and the one that those in charge of teams, most notably coaches, are quickest to bemoan. Can you genuinely tell me that the successful 2005 and 2008 Grand Slam Welsh players are any less or any more capable than those in 2004, 2006 and 2007? That the England players at the start of the 2007 World Cup (where we had nobody of world class, apparently) were different in ability from those who narrowly lost the final a few weeks later? The point is that at such levels, where in terms of fitness, size, strength, skill, desire and all the other components the teams are effectively equal, it is how a team is run, operated, coached and managed that makes the difference.

That said, no manager, leader or coach can account for individual brilliance or failure. If you have a Barry John, a Waisale Serevi or a Dan Cipriani in your team there is always the possibility that you'll have a touch of genius that is uncoachable.

Sometimes, if you've made a mistake, your team has lost or you've had a shocker, you hate yourself. Very rarely, though, will it be through lack of effort either during the game or beforehand in training – it's just the inevitability of sport. Sportsmen are human: they make mistakes. It's just that on the sports field your mistakes are more visible, more obvious than those that people make in everyday life. But mistakes need to be kept in perspective;

they're not a matter of life or death – although they can sometimes feel as if they are – and at such times it really is important to have other things, people and interests in your life as otherwise you'd probably go mad. The key to coping with mistakes is to treat them as impostors.

If a few individuals in a team let their confidence drop, it can rapidly become contagious and collective self-doubt can shape a bad result on the day. Moves that on any other occasion would flow easily just don't come off. Individual technical errors multiply and there seems to be an inevitability about the game's outcome. An example of this was the snowballing of execution and technical errors that plagued Wasps' early 08/09 season. Physically the players are the same, but mentally and emotionally they've shifted. How the squad responds is a real test of the leadership of managers, coaches and players themselves – leadership that builds emotional resilience for when things start to go against you both individually and collectively, and which quickly takes hold of the situation to restore a winning performance. Another example to contrast with the above was the Wales win over England in the 2008 Six Nations. The first-half performance by England was in many ways ominous. The pundits at half time even predicted the opening of floodgates, yet the transition in composure and confidence was stark, resulting eventually in, quite frankly, a staggering turn-around of events.

Life's easy when you're playing well, but when you're not you have to be able to take it on the chin, face up to it and move on. It's how you come back that is the mark of your character. After a bad game you want to play the next day to put it right. The key to getting your form back is not to over-analyse, to try not to spend any time outside training thinking about rugby, to be humble, to admit when you're wrong, to not worry about other people's jobs, to maintain the same level of unyielding commitment and determination, to work specifically on what's let you down and, the hardest part, to be patient. And never, ever, let those little demons of self-doubt grind you down! There are times in your life when those around you doubt you, when even those closest to you or care most for you lack belief in you. They might say all the right things and go through the motions, but you can see it in their eyes. It's then that you are most on your own, facing the biggest challenge. In hindsight during my career I've probably experienced such moments on a few occasions, at which point you find out then where people's loyalty really lies. You're by yourself but, as always, the tide does turn! Being pragmatic about things helps. Sometimes after you've played well you watch your game again and become a bit deflated when you realise that you aren't after all the messiah resurrected; conversely, after playing badly, you may find that you have judged what was actually a good performance on a couple of mistakes.

Early in the 2008–9 season, playing Northampton, I had an absolutely shocking start to a game, having my kick charged down in the opening minute for the opposition to score. I had taken too long, made a technical error and so was the first to put my hand up to apologise to the rest of the lads. Ten minutes later a high ball was put up and being rooted by the kick (that is, I had to stay where I was to catch it rather than move forward to it) I jumped as high as I could to take the ball, but without protection (your other players running blocking lines), the six-foot-four opposition centre jumped higher than I did and tapped the ball. It bounced off the ground and into the hands of one of their team who ran under the sticks. Physically there was nothing else I could have done, and technically I hadn't made a mistake; it was just a case of a good kick and an excellent chase by the other team. Inevitably, though, people watching think that you've 'dropped it' and all of a sudden you're having a shocker, appearing to have lost confidence under the high ball. I played well for the rest of the game but that didn't matter. I sat in the dressing room, head in my hands with a face that suggested I'd just shot the family pet. I was asked afterwards by one of the least popular rugby journalists, 'Was that the worst game of your life?' This was the same guy who a few months earlier had said I was the best full back in the world. Where is the sensible middle-ground?

Players can also develop their own leadership, management and coaching roles but again the key to that is getting the right balance between those doing it in an official capacity. In my experience, good players can bail you out of trouble when it matters most. When every other element of a game is substandard, good, determined players can often turn the tide. However, over a prolonged period or an entire season, if these elements are not properly in place there will generally be underachievement, an unhappy camp and frustrated individuals. Without naming sides and thus implicating specific individuals it doesn't take a brain surgeon to work out when this has occurred.

In short, the players are at the heart of any successful sports team. Without enough quality, the future success of the setup is hypothetical, but to my mind too much is made of the difference in playing standards. In writing this book I have come to the conclusion that, with the odd exception, there is practically nothing to distinguish between the top sixty players in the Premiership; it is just how well they're managed, coached, led and their perceived current form. To that end, with the new England setup, the Premiership clubs all playing scintillating, high-intensity stuff and the main man at the helm who knows a thing or two about leadership and management, let's hope that we're witnessing the dawn of a very exciting time for English rugby.

Chapter 15

Mountains and Travel

'**W**ELL, IT'S NOT EXACTLY Ibiza, but it'll be more memorable and you might even impress some birds with your stinky chat for a change . . .' I said.

'Just as long as you don't sing your bloody country and western shite,' Keith replied.

'Don't get me wrong, I've got broad shoulders, but I'm not carrying your sorry arse for three whole -weeks.'

'Fine, but if you pinch my food, you're dead.'

That was it. Decision made – K2 here we come.

My brothers had been in 2004, two years earlier, I had the summer off and, having never had the opportunity to travel properly as many of my friends and contemporaries had in their gap years, I was keen at least to see and experience a little of what I had missed. Cue Pakistan's North-West Frontier – geographically wild, barren and beautiful, ideologically and culturally fascinating. I'd always wanted to visit the country of origin of many of the lads

I'd gone to school with at Watford GS, and with so many of the world's ills apparently stemming from the ideological clash between Christianity and Islam, rather than form my opinions from television or newspapers I was keen to see an Islamic republic for myself. The Everest route through Nepal had become incredibly commercial and it didn't have the same appeal; the pared-down nature of the Karakoram, before it too became entirely Westernised, was more intriguing. Lastly, one of my all-time heroes, that quintessential English gentleman Michael Palin, had recently highlighted the Baltoro Glacier and the Pakistan side of the region, in his TV series *Himalaya*, and so, along with seeing the world's greatest peaks, following in his footsteps was good enough for me.

The politically sensitive area was rated as risky by the Foreign Office – a bit dangerous but not totally off limits. Keith and I rigged ourselves up with a no-frills mountaineering operator who sent a representative from the UK to join the two of us and liaise with the small team of local porters. We landed in Islamabad, a cheeky 35 degrees Celsius, at 0400 hours, and that was the first taste of the humour, chaos and lawlessness that in many ways typified the entire trip. It was four in the morning and yet children were already out on the streets playing cricket; there must have been a thousand or so people waiting at the airport, not to meet anyone apparently but just to watch. There certainly didn't seem to be any form of queuing system, more a case of push, crowd and shout.

My travelling companion, old army friend and future joint best man, Keith Reesby, started the trip both horrified and in hysterics as we watched the actions of the luggage porters. Shouting at each other or bellowing into the mouthpiece of a mobile phone, they were throwing the bags from the hold of the 747 out on a looping arc to crash on to the tarmac thirty feet below. Regular visitors to Islamabad will also notice that the only advertisement in the entire airport is for a curry house in Bradford! Despite this robust handling, all our luggage turned up present and correct and we were met by our kind, tough and loyal head guide Mashur and taken to the hostel where we'd stay the first night.

We were obviously keen to see some of the real Islamabad and, it being too hot to sleep, we swiftly went to a local market followed by a visit to the country's largest mosque. In comparison to some of the more regional backwaters Islamabad is, with its manicured lawns, presidential and governmental buildings, a developed, cosmopolitan and, in some places, opulent oasis. Glamorous women strolled in the shopping arcades and though most wore a headscarf out of respect for their religion, there did seem to be a genuine air of tolerance and, as in most large cities, a flagrant lack of interest in other people's affairs.

We were told that shorts were fine for us to wear, though (and I quote) 'not Speedos'!

'That's you buggered then, mate,' Keith said – predictable if nothing else.

I bought a pair of flip-flops for the equivalent of 50p and the man seemed so happy with the deal that I couldn't bring myself to bother bartering over another 5p. Slightly further along, the first example of the local food and hygiene regulations reared its head. A local butcher was carving up a freshly slaughtered goat, and strips of meat were hanging from the ceiling, drying in the midday sun. There was the obligatory swarm of flies around the hanging meat and on the carcass. Not being the squeamish type it didn't bother me, but I was a little surprised to hear that the discarded heads that lay in the gutter along with the waste and human excrement would most certainly not be wasted. 'Pakistan soup!' Mashur proudly proclaimed.

Though being brought up in a house with two hungry brothers where you turned your back on your plate at your peril, I was nonetheless paranoid about getting ill and for the first time in my life thought about the food I was about to eat before digging in.

Dad would blithely scrape off the layer of fur from the top of a yoghurt and scones without the odd spore just weren't home-made, so, not being the fussiest person, I'd like to think that I had a fairly healthy and natural level of immunity, but coming from a culture where even my good lady sometimes confuses her left and right hands, I wasn't entirely convinced of the merits of one hand for wiping, the other for eating! Although I run the risk of sounding like a spoiled, uncultured snob, I was fully aware that perhaps two-thirds of the globe ate in this way, but when the first alfresco fondue was presented, and our local guide's eyes welled up with pride, I hadn't the heart to offend. It nonetheless felt like a massive leap of faith.

Talking of faith, there are few places in the world where this would be tested more than on the ancient silk route connecting Pakistan to China – the infamous Karakoram Highway, mile upon endless mile carved out of the side of the mountain. Our driver was affectionately known as 'Allah G', as the stickers on the windscreen and rear windows proclaimed. Our vehicle was, in comparison to the broad array of 'jingly buses', a fairly sedate and dull minivan. Anyone who's travelled to the region will be familiar with the colour and vibrancy with which drivers decorate their vehicles. Lorries are laden with tons of equipment, with hundreds of people hanging from every imaginable part or grabbing a lift from one place to another. The Highway Code seems to be that priority goes to the biggest vehicle. That's well and good, but, although I'm not the religious type, when you're on a motorway and someone is coming at you doing 50mph on the wrong side of the road, or there's no safety barrier on a dirt track twenty-foot wide with a thousand-foot drop and your worn-out tyres have got no tread, or a twenty-ton lorry careers towards you around a blind bend with a driver who hasn't slept for two days – well, you begin to understand why you'd find a need to pray five times a day.

It was an experience in itself. It is said that the Karakoram Highway is the highest as well as the most dangerous road in the world. Whether or not the latter is true, the graveyard of rusting vehicles visible in the valley below certainly made for a nail-biting trip. Being the main artery of trade and travel, there were of course some amazing towns and villages along this varied route. We'd enter one town fully used to Westerners, able to cater for our commercial tastes and reassure us with brand names; others made it quite clear that they did not welcome infidels, so much so that even our guide told us to stay out of sight.

It was a revealing insight into the region's geography and nature. One morning, the road was blocked by an avalanche a few hundred yards from where we had stopped. Large boulders were strewn all over the road and the odd rock the size of a human head plummeted down to the valley below. To be fair, the local road maintenance boys were on the case – a ten-year-old kid was sitting in the middle of the highway waving a red flag!

It appeared that each section of the highway was regulated and maintained by the nearest town or village – they needed it the most for passing trade and the contact it brought them. The toughness of these mountain people soon began to strike you: in this hard, barren landscape, they had grooved, carved and forged irrigation trenches, created plateaux and reared livestock on what would otherwise be impossible terrain. We found an interesting correlation between the amount of greenery a place had and the number of women and children present. The lush grass and tilled, fertile soil were synonymous with bright colours, relative wealth, children playing and women singing as they tended their crops – life appeared to be vibrant and cheerful. The valley was cut by the great Indus River, with the majority of the vibrant villages positioned on the opposite side of the river to the road in order to make most use of what little sun penetrated the valley. Such pockets of colour, vegetation and apparent prosperity amongst the sparse, bleak and intimidating peaks seemed in some way to be magical little hidden kingdoms. Some of them, reaching up from the river front right into the clouds, reminded me of Rivendell from Tolkien's *Lord of the Rings*. In such an unforgiving, cruel terrain such places appeared almost mythical – protected by the mountains as lush havens for all that was good.

However, there was the odd stop that appeared entirely more sinister, dark and forbidding. You were distinctly not welcome in such places, where not a blade of grass grew, where there wasn't the smallest semblance of happiness. Women and children were either absent altogether or kept firmly out of sight. At one such stop both Keith and I remarked on the piercing, emotionless, haunted look of a young girl staring at us from the shadows of a distant building. We were reliably informed that such places were strongholds of the mujahideen or the Taliban. Pakistan was run by the military. Whether it was popular or not, at the time it was widely considered that under his direction President General Musharraf was able to get things organised and maintain some level of order. It would be an international embarrassment and a PR nightmare if this route, often used by Westerners like us, was in any way not controlled and regulated by the pro-Western Pakistani forces. As such, and in addition to the turbulent issues of Kashmir, there was a regular and persistent military presence along the route. Without it, such stops in hostile villages, and in fact probably the whole trip, would not have been possible. Though it was highly unlikely, with Keith being a serving army pilot there was always the unnerving possibility of being kidnapped.

'Oh my word, this place is the real deal,' Keith would say.

'That's it. I'm going to tell him that you've shot his mates.'

'Fine, but when I'm having my head sawn off you've got to explain it to my mum!'

Keith had already had 'a spot of bother', as he describes it, having been shot in Iraq earlier. His dry, sardonic humour was always an amusing tonic for my impulsive enthusiasm. He takes after his father, Phil, being intelligent but reserved, preferring, as all proper English males do, to keep his own counsel particularly on embarrassing matters like emotions. Keith is a man who once famously shook a girl by the hand to say goodbye after a night together. I, of course, find such awkwardness hilarious.

Having been shot through the chest and arm, with only his dog tags stopping the bullet hitting his heart, once stabilised, like all good boys he was eager to put his parents' minds at ease. When your son is on operations and has been wounded, if the first voice you hear isn't his, it must be a terrible shock to the system. For that reason he asked if he could ring his parents back in the UK to let them know what had happened and that he was going to be OK.

His nurses found his emergency contact number, which, during working hours, was his father's place of work.

'Hi, Dad, it's Keith.'

'Hello, Keith, strange of you to call me at work.' (Keith hadn't called his father there in twenty-five years.)

'Well, Dad, I've had quite a strange day as it happens – I've been shot! But it's OK, I'm now going to be fine, and they'll probably be sending me home in a few days.'

Pause.

'Right then . . . I'll be sure to tell your mother. Bye now.'

Quite clearly the apple doesn't fall far from the tree, but a constant source of amusement he certainly is and if we were to be kidnapped and brutally decapitated, there are few others who would take it so well!

We finally arrived in Skardu which supported a huge military base and was the last town before the real trekking started. We were told that we were to be one of the very first groups on to the glacier that season and definitely the first to cross the Gondogoro La Pass as the snow was still too thick for the fixed ropes to be put in and avalanche risk was high.

We had a night in a hostel and time to reflect before the proper job of putting one foot in front of the other started. In my diary I wrote about how so far in this alien environment I'd been humbled and impressed by the people. They were, as expected, by and large very welcoming folk, all having a reasonable grasp of English and a willingness to learn more, but most striking of all was their toughness and resilience and the way they got on with things without fuss. Years of living in relative poverty and harsh surroundings have made them into a practical people, unspoiled by luxury. There appeared to us to be a top-line communal moral disapproval of the West and some of its values, but below that line a personal interest and a certain intrigue in its delights and comforts. We referred to it as the 'Americans go home, but take me with you' philosophy.

The following morning we embarked by 4 × 4 along a ridiculous road to the village of Askoli, perhaps the most northerly village in Pakistan. The driver was a cheerful and loud man with a horrendous voice and as far as the car was concerned, presumably suspension was an optional extra. Never having had the opportunity to travel to really remote parts of the globe, for me Askoli was one of the highlights of the trip. There were children everywhere, and as we were the first Westerners they'd seen in months, we were followed around the village like the Pied Piper. Keith and I cheerfully and with great enjoyment went straight into a 'Hearts and Minds' role, giving out sweets, taking photos and joining in with various games of kabadi. It was brilliant and gave us both an uplifting send-off for the following weeks of graft.

'Time spent on reconnaissance is seldom wasted' apparently, so in typical fashion neither Keith nor I had even tried on our footwear outside Cotswold's (the shop, not the hilly region) and, in terms of endurance, we'd spent precisely no time whatsoever acclimatising ourselves to long days of plodding under the pretext of 'don't be soft – we'll be reet!'. Unsurprisingly, being the admin vortexes we both were, it took a few days for us to adjust to the routine of packing up, bedding down, tending to feet etc.

On the first morning we'd been told in no uncertain terms that we were to leave by five, having had a decent breakfast. We needn't have worried about waking up on time. Despite the remote backwater of the glacial ravine we found ourselves in, the first call to prayer was Tannoyed up the valley from the nearest village a few miles to the south. That was it: chickens, goats and finally a huge donkey only feet from our tent thought it time to start exercising their vocal cords at 0300 hours.

It'd been a while since either of us had done the tent-share thing and with Keith 'danger, Special K, admin ninja, flexibility' Reesby getting the squits early doors, it was a fairly ominous sign for the rest of the trip, not to mention for his sleeping bag. With regard to the trekking it was usually around 30 degrees C during the day on the approach and lower levels of the glacier, obviously becoming freezing at night and colder the higher you went.

It became clear very early on that, having little or no training and with such demands, albeit simply those of walking, it was to be a fair old amount of graft to reach base camp and the pass.

The level of exercise is one thing – anyone reasonably fit would be able to manage it – but along with the high altitude, sleeping arrangements and monotonous food, fatigue builds up and saps your morale, making the whole process that much harder. We, of course, were just soft and had become pampered by the lives we led. Being a professional sportsman I was used to the correct food, nutrition and rest as and when I needed it. Keith, now mostly doing a desk-bound job and allegedly a 'power' athlete, struggled just as much. My brother Tom had said that food would be plentiful but lacking in variety and quality and recommended that we buy a goat to take with us to ensure we had sufficient protein, as the higher we went the less fresh and varied the diet. I very much enjoy my fresh fruit and veg back home, so to do without for the best part of three weeks, on top of the debilitating altitude, left me lethargic and under-enthused. Breakfast was usually at 0500 hours, lunch about 0100 and dinner at 1800, before bed at 2000.

The food was predominantly either freshly made chapattis or hunza bread. This stuff was the very antithesis of the Atkins Diet, having the same periodic table value as lead and probably amazing for absorbing industrial leakages, but in our dehydrated state and with our dry mouths it was challenging stuff. Lastly, the staple diet was goat soup. Your mind went back to the slurry outside the butchers in Islamabad, but this wasn't the place to start getting picky. What exactly they did with the actual meat is a good question as, apart from the meat-flavoured broth, the only recognisable part of the animal was the odd shard of tooth or spine. 'Mmm! Delicious. My favourite – goat lips again!'

In truth, the porters providing the food were absolute stars. They were working for about 50p a day, grafting their backsides off carrying the majority of the camp's weight in the most difficult of circumstances, providing plenty of edible food that was both imaginative and well put together, considering the lack of fresh ingredients or facilities. At difficult moments or those that challenged morale, you only had to look at our weathered porters – some in their fifties, half our weight, but carrying twice as much, in return for what? Tuppence a day, three grains of rice and a goat's eyeball.

These were hard men. In many ways they reminded me of my grandfather's generation. Dadgu worked every day of his adult life down the mines, toiling with pickaxe, hammer and chisel, chipping away at the anthracite in South Wales to make ends meet. It was what was expected and what everyone from the Cwmllynfell and the surrounding areas did. It wasn't for material wealth but just enough to get by, provide for the family and afford a couple of beers watching the rugby come Saturday afternoon. We, in comparison, have become spoiled and soft.

These guys could savour a five-minute break as their one enjoyment of the day; they sent any savings back to their families and would huddle together under a rug on rocks, with just a flimsy piece of tarpaulin keeping the snow off as temperatures plummeted at night to minus-30 degrees C. We therefore agreed not to whinge no matter how minging we felt our predicament to be; embarrassingly, we had state-of-the-art tents, down sleeping bags and expensive footwear.

The porters' clothing amazed me. Here were folk whose job it was to clamber up and down an undulating mass of scree and boulders all season long and even after we gave them our kit as a tip at the end of the trip they preferred to sell it and use their own – this comprised home-made backpacks held together with fencing wire, a rug which doubled up for warmth at night and to keep the sun off during the day, socks and sandals (with plastic bags wrapped around them if it got wet, their version of crampons being to put yet another coarse pair of socks over the top to give them a grip on the snow!) instead of boots. Being able to survive for years on end with little expectation from life on such meagre rations of food or material reward, it wasn't surprising that for centuries their ancestors, the hardy Pathan tribesmen of the North-West Frontier, and the rugged terrain they inhabited, had been impossible to tame.

Trekking amongst the world's highest peaks, with unbelievable panoramas, we should have been awe-struck by the splendour and content and satisfied with our daily lot. The reality, of course, was quite different. When you are working hard for hours on end, it is all too easy to fall into a trance-like state, staring down to see where you put your next footstep. It was bizarre but on some of our longest days – twelve to fourteen hours on the go – you'd sometimes be no more than three yards from each other and yet not utter a word till you stopped for lunch or evening camp. Neither of us wanted to be negative, and despite the cheerful claims of 'This is shit!' or 'I'm choosing next year's holiday', you were determined to keep quiet, not wanting to be the one to moan or allow the other to think that you were 'hanging out'. For all the joking and teasing, I've never been scared of a bit of hard work and Keith is a tough bastard himself, but with the lack of prep and other mitigating circumstances, in all honesty it was the hardest thing either of us had ever done. It may seem bizarre to some people that, only a few yards apart, you can nonetheless go for hours on end without speaking, but talking necessitates conscious thought and things seem to take longer when you are actually thinking. Your mind quickly acquires the ability to turn off for hours, to 'zone out' or 'switch off', to blot out the monotonous pain and lethargy brought about by pushing yourself at altitude.

The things you hold dearest tend to float in and out of your consciousness. You're closer to your natural limits and, as such, your innate, instinctive feelings are heightened. It's great for decision-making. Often when we try to see both sides of an argument, being reasonable and tolerant we tend to sit on the fence, to settle for the grey area. In the position we now found ourselves in, life and its choices appeared far clearer – they were black or white. Perhaps in such circumstances you have too much time to think, to worry about whether or not you should be mentally going in a particular direction. However, I've always been a dreamer, an idealist, and as such have always set my goals accordingly to make such things a reality. Reality is, of course, far more boring and is very rarely as good as the dream, but the anticipation itself is enough to get me out of bed every morning to at least try and achieve those dreams. I thought about all sorts of things but, most significantly, where I saw my life going, where I wanted to be, and most of all how I wanted to feel.

Home has always been a big thing for me. Since I was a little boy I'd dreamed of a house in the country, with my own family, dogs at my feet, perhaps some pigs and chickens too. Teaching your boy to fish and shoot or attending ballet class with your girl, telling stories by the fire or fighting over Sunday lunch – they're not rock and roll but balanced with life's more racy yet vacuous pleasures they are what matter to me. So I borrowed a satellite phone and rang my girlfriend, Vanessa.

It is in such circumstances that you learn most about yourself, I believe. Your mind finds clarity when at other times decision-making can be more complicated. Thoughts become more polarised as you test your physical capabilities, your heightened natural instincts take over, being divorced from the noise and artificiality of modern society.

There were times when Keith or I would start a conversation just to break the monotony of walking, but my attempts at Garth Brooks, Christy Moore or Kenny Rogers would exasperate him even more. There are, of course, times when you fall out, run out of things to say, or simply don't want to talk at all. What fascinates me, however, is how aspects of psychology and leadership can be beneficial to each other, especially the lessons we take from nature. A simple analogy of this would be when someone tries to start a conversation with you when you're 'hanging out' on a treadmill in the gym. And if someone is doing the same speed as you on a treadmill next to you, laughing, and chatting away, it just makes you feel worse in comparison.

A flight of geese will travel vast distances as they migrate each year so, as peloton cyclists have learned, they fly in formation to create a more aerodynamic flight pattern, regularly changing the front-flying bird, with the birds at the back having the most impact and determining the overall speed of the flight. This brings to mind one of my greatest heroes, Sir Ranulph Fiennes, who wrote in his book *Beyond the Limits* about the relationship he had on expeditions with his good friend Dr Mike Stroud. Interestingly, Fiennes and Stroud would take turns in being the point man. There is always something liberating about being at the front. As well as leading physically, you feel you are mentally ahead of the others. Conversely, being at the back can have a negative effect; you're 'just keeping up' or trailing behind. Both men found that taking turns at point was immeasurably useful in helping them to maintain a positive mindset and a solid performance. There is something almost primeval about seeing others suffer. No matter how tired or how bad you feel, seeing someone else struggling more than you is in some way uplifting, as you think, 'Well, he's worse off than me'. My easiest day coincided with Keith finally losing his sense of humour and taking a swipe at our considerate guide, and Keith's face erupted into the broadest of grins the day I woke up with facial oedema while also discharging liquid from both ends.

We achieved our goal of reaching K2 base camp at over 5,000 metres. We didn't, however, go over the pass as the risk of avalanche was deemed too great, and it took all the persuasive powers of Keith and our English guide, Zac Poulton, in a real team effort, to convince me that, in my incapacitated state, it would be foolish to attempt it. And so, after a day at the foot of the world's most savage mountain, we said goodbye to the globe's biggest glaciers and to Concordia, where they all meet – translated as 'the high throne of the mountain gods' – and retraced our steps.

On the way back down, the air becoming noticeably richer and with energy surging back into our bodies, we stopped at one of the purpose-built camps that cater for the new stream of trekkers, sensibly avoiding the dirt, rubbish and ruined landscape that have become synonymous with the Everest circus. Being the first trekkers of the season, we had seen few others on the route, but on the way back we were afforded a glimpse of the commercial future of that region. Hundreds of climbers, accompanied by thousands of porters, were making the same trip up as we had. Some, like us, were simply trekking; others were intent on scaling the 8,000-metre giants, and a chosen few were attempting to reach and climb the holy grail itself – K2, the 'savage mountain'. Unlike Everest, there is no established route to the summit. Only being a couple of hundred metres lower, K2 is technically far more difficult to climb and, frighteningly, has taken one in four of those who have reached the summit. One such climber we met was Gerry McDonnell from Limerick. His team, Munster, had just deservedly won the Heineken Cup and with him on guitar we attempted a very poor rendition of Christy Moore's 'Little Musgrave'. I was struck not just by his energy and enthusiasm but by the fact that he'd moved out to Alaska a few years back, purely to train in order to climb K2. For the first time I began to understand the extraordinary allure and mystique of climbing such indomitable mountains. Gerry failed that first year, not getting a suitable weather window, and it was with great sadness that I learned that he was one of the eleven climbers who lost their lives in August 2008, on the descent, after realising his dream.

A good old rugby friend of mine and university pal of Keith's worked for the Foreign Office in Islamabad and had a large house in the diplomatic enclave that he kindly invited us to stay at. To be honest, the house could have been a coal shed and it would have appeared luxurious, but the sudden culture clash was quite startling. Twenty-four hours earlier we'd been living off screech (a powdered squash drink used in the army) and dried bread. We arrived at the house unshaven, dirty and soiled and within five minutes had a cold beer in our hands and were watching Sky television.

Humans are incredibly resourceful and adaptable. We don't like getting out of bed and going out into the cold. We prefer hot water to wash with and a fridge with cool, fresh food. However, if they're not available, or if we don't know of anything else, then comforts, luxuries and treats become relative. For the porters who accompanied us, comfort meant having time for a fag, or a day without snow; for us it meant a day with solid stools. Although such relative values are quickly forgotten when we go back to our soft, pampered lives, I think they're good to revisit every so often. They remind us of who we really are.

Chapter 16

Hobbies and Pastimes

BEN ELTON'S NOVEL *Chart Throb* – his satirical look at our national obsession with fame and celebrity through the likes of *The X Factor* and *Pop Idol* – concerns the story of a certain white-toothed, media-savvy genius, Calvin Simms, who bets that the antithesis of the industry – the dignified, moral and genuine Prince of Wales, who, unlike many, hasn't taken the PR and media middle-ground – could win the reality show competition in question. Unsurprisingly, the manipulation is in the editing and to ensure that he peaks at the right moment, and not too early, after initial success and surging popularity as viewers begin to understand more about this often misrepresented individual, Simms puts the brakes on the prince by bringing up the fox-hunting/shooting angle: 'No matter what the reasons, no matter how logical or justified, what I do know is that the British public do not like seeing furry animals being killed!' The editing has the desired effect and the prince slips back down the ratings.

Somewhat tentatively, therefore, I am going to touch on my passions outside rugby and so it would be remiss of me not to mention my love of country sports, outdoor pursuits and surfing.

Surfing is so natural. To say that it's a form of escapism is an understatement. More practically, when you've got hundreds of tons of water about to crash down on top of you, there are more pressing matters than the mundane stresses and chores that we get so worked up about in daily life. Without attempting to sound like some sort of hippy, it is a great way of putting things into perspective. Feeling the awesome power and beauty of the ocean you are quickly reminded how insignificant you are in the grand scheme of things. That's the wishy-washy, spiritual stuff out of the way. It is also an amazing adrenalin rush, catching the wave at the crest, having just got up enough speed and then riding the wave down and along its face. You're probably only travelling a few miles an hour but at the time it feels incredibly fast. I'm talking as if I'm some sort of seasoned pro. I am, of course, crap, but with the exhilaration and excitement blended with sheer adrenalin and the endorphins generated from lots of paddling, afterwards, wrapped up with a hot drink or a slowly inebriating apple rattler in hand, there are few greater feelings of contentment.

Outdoor pursuits and surfing are things that don't cause controversy – well, not for the moment anyway, not until some politically correct body deems it too 'outdoorist' to actually enjoy anything apart from urban coffee shops and wine bars. Without turning a chapter on hobbies and pastimes into some sort of polemic and rambling on about why I support the hunting/shooting/fishing fraternity – in general a well-regulated and morally decent bunch – it may be worth summarising a few general points.

On such emotive subjects as hunting and shooting in particular, misjudged but sometimes instinctive reactions often override reasoned logic, and, indeed, I myself once disapproved of such pastimes. However, having now been educated into their ways, and having met the sort of people involved and experienced for myself their procedures and practices, I'm now a staunch supporter of such rural activities.

You only have to leave bin bags out overnight to realise that both urban and rural fox populations have exploded thanks to modern society's invasive presence. This may not be of so much importance to the flat-dwelling masses in large cities, but ask any farmer who keeps livestock and he will soon explain the necessity of culling foxes. I have known farmers who regularly work twenty hours a days, seven days a week, just to make ends meet so that their farms can be passed on to the next generation. For them to lose even more revenue than they already are to foxes is devastating. Perhaps one of the key questions is: what is the most humane method of controlling the fox population?

Some people believe shooting to be the answer. With fox-hunting with dogs being banned, anybody licensed to own a shotgun or rifle can now go out and commit their own form of culling, often leaving injured foxes to die slow, painful deaths. There will be no form of natural selection, as in hunting, where the weakest are killed. This way fit males, pregnant vixens and cubs will be killed or, worse, wounded. How about the classic nineteenth-century methods of snaring or poisoning? Again, both are indiscriminate and death is agonising and slow.

I am the owner of two beautiful, gentle dogs, but it is obvious to me that they are by nature pack animals and that their most basic instinct is to hunt. Fox-hunting merely allows this to occur and provides with it a form of natural selection. A fit, healthy fox can run about 25mph. The larger foxhound tops out at about 20mph. Therefore, fox-hunting weeds out the old, lame or sick foxes – which are the ones most likely to artificially extend their lives by living off the by-products of human existence, such as livestock or edible waste. While the kill itself may be quite gruesome and understandably upsetting to witness, it is usually the quickest form of death for an animal in the wild.

Many objections to hunting are made not on the manner of death but in the belief that human beings revel in it. This is not the case. In fact, most of the men, women and children who hunt are animal lovers. Every huntsman I have met would prefer not to kill a fox at all if that meant inflicting a slow, agonising death. But critics should realise that fox-hunting is a fact of nature, a part of rural life and the rural economy, and, importantly, a social event. Politicians frequently mention how the social problems in our society are largely a result of the reduction of the sense of community. Therefore such social gatherings in rural areas are vital in helping to retain a sense of entity and belonging. I believe this is particularly the case as the numbers attending church continue to decline.

It seems to me that, if the evidence from various chat shows and so-called 'informed' debates is anything to go on, many people who supported the ban on fox-hunting thought it would affect only the 'aristocracy' or 'toffs', and that fox-hunting is a sport undertaken exclusively by the upper class. In fact, the people most affected would be those likely to lose their jobs, the people who look after the hounds and prepare the horses, shoe them, feed them, harness them, and so on.

The stark reality is that without hunting in some form, most of the hounds will have to be put down since they are working animals and do not make suitable pets. The breeding, bloodlines and background of all these dogs will be lost, as will ancillary events such as point-to-point meetings.

But for me the saddest aspect is that one of the most traditional, distinctive and iconic sights, one that has taken place for generations – the gathering of riders and hounds at a meet – will no longer be seen in the beautiful British countryside.

On a day off I love nothing better than to take out my beloved boys (two boxer dogs) and work them, flushing or picking up. They are both the most docile and loving animals, but they are at their most natural and happiest when running free in a field of maize, the closest thing to what they would do naturally in the wild. They are, of course, not natural gun dogs, and in comparison to well-drilled Labs and spaniels almost hopeless – one won't even pick up at all – but the reward you get from the bond with an animal that you've trained, loved and watched perform is better than any good shot you make or trophy you collect. Am I not an animal lover? In all honesty I spoil them and am probably a little soft; I find it difficult to treat them purely as working dogs as fundamentally they are pets, first and foremost. If you are a full-time farmer or shepherd, your dog is your most trusted companion and your trade's most important tool. I've found that even the toughest and most pragmatic of farmers or rural types have a soft spot for the animals they keep and nurture.

Reading the books by the great James Herriot, it seems that even the hardiest and driest-witted Yorkshire farmers, who understood the cycle of life and death in nature better than most, would always favour a certain animal, or show kindness and a softer side even to livestock that they'd raised. As such you treat them with respect and dignity – a far cry from the pampered accessories with their pink overcoats and 'dog jewellery' that you see in the streets around west London or in Paris. It's not my position to criticise, because a dog, cat or other pet provides companionship for many elderly, lonely people. But which are the more unruly? Dogs are pack animals, and I've never seen a pampered pooch in a pink duffel coat come promptly to heel, or work lovingly for the attention of its master and friend.

My grandfather preferred animals to human beings and, like most countrymen, he understood the delicate balance of the ecosystem and its needs. Unfortunately, thanks to mankind's presence on this crowded earth, where some species have blossomed others have dwindled. Consequently, aligned with an agrarian philosophy, in order to maintain a healthy environment it is important to redress the balance that our lifestyle has had on the ecology around us. Take deer, for example. The British Deer Society, a registered charity of which I'm a member, along with the Rare Breeds Survival Trust and the Countryside Alliance, looks to maintain the gradual and sustainable growth of the deer population. I look after land for some folk in Buckinghamshire on which the indigenous roe deer is more scarce than its more resilient, territorial and aggressive oriental cousin, the muntjac. Because of the huge damage the muntjac can do to the flora and fauna, which then impacts on insect and bird life and in that way continues to affect the rest of the local ecosystem, I shoot them to manage their numbers, not to eradicate them but to allow the plants and trees and the other animals around them to thrive and so maintain a healthy woodland. We are, thankfully, beginning to see the 'ghost of the forest' – our indigenous roe deer – returning too. The same issue exists with many other animals here, the grey squirrel and American crayfish being two obvious examples.

Through the larger registered charities and regulatory bodies, the shooting fraternity, aware of the bitter resentment and discriminatory behaviour of our urbanised government – and aware that its prejudiced focus of attention will soon turn from the 'toffs' of fox-hunting to other rural pastimes – has rightly commissioned its own, independent research into gauging public opinion so that it can move in the right direction and ensure that its civil liberties are protected. Research shows that woodlands or lands that are shot on, and thus managed, are statistically more likely to have greater biodiversity, and thus be healthier, than those that are not. In layman's terms, when you walk through a wood and hear the dawn chorus it's songbirds that are providing this – not scavengers like magpies or crows whose population, if left uncontrolled, will explode. The CA commissioned the biggest research project into public attitudes in recent times, called 'Attitudes to Shooting'. In the study a succession of focus groups attended by a diverse cross-section of people found that there were three main reasons why the public would support shooting: food, its potential role as an economic driver in a harsh rural climate and accessibility for more people. Amazingly, although the whole question of conservation is at the top of many shooters' list, it holds little sway with the public, although it is still a vital political card as parties jostle for the green vote. For anyone who wants to take this debate further, I would recommend the 2007 Man Asian Literary Prize winner, *Wolf Totem*, by Jiang Rong, an educational novel that touches on the complex interrelationship between nomads and settlers, animals and humans, nature and culture.

Economically, the rural community has had a tough time of late with DEFRA and other overly bureaucratic bodies crippling an already struggling farming community. The CA found that the public accepted the need for diversification so that farmers could make ends meet and, to that end, would accept shooting as a way of doing this. Independently, acccording to a 2006 economic and environmental report funded by a number of shooting bodies, shooting is worth £1.6 billion to the rural economy and supports more than 70,000 jobs in this country. However, the one justification for shooting that is most notably agreed upon and accepted is that it can provide an ethical and healthy source of food. Mark Malins' research with the Department of Social and Policy Sciences at University of Bath, which was reported in the British Deer Society Journal in 2007 found that 81 per cent of those surveyed either agreed or strongly agreed that landowners should be able to sell venison themselves. He also found that 69 per cent either agreed or strongly agreed with the principal of deer control. The Countryside Alliance Game-to-Eat campaign, along with other initiatives, has seen sales in game increase by 64 per cent since 2002, and according to an independent report by Mintel, the market is now worth £69 million. With the exception of vermin (which I shoot in a desperate attempt to keep numbers down), I either eat, sell to the butcher or trade all that I shoot for consumption, and I know of very few people who kill animals for any other reason. Game, as everyone knows, is pretty much the healthiest and most natural form of meat, nutritionally packed, wild, and thus as 'free range' as you can get.

But what about the actual killing itself? Understandably few people either enjoy this process or like seeing it done. Seeing any animal suffering is unpleasant and is one of the things that really touches our emotions. We all like to see nature at its most gentle – the doe nuzzling its fawn, cute-eyed pups play-fighting, or the heart-wrenching signs of affection between a wild animal and its mate. The reality is, of course, that the polar opposite of such behaviour also exists. A domestic cat will tease and torture not for food but amusement. A sparrowhawk will mutilate any smaller bird it can find; the same wolf pack that shows paternal instincts can cruelly turn on its weakest member. This is also natural. So what part do we play in this circle of life? Undoubtedly we are responsible for many, many examples of unjustified, ill-considered and unregulated cruelty. I for one do not agree with huge drive days where hundreds and hundreds of birds are flushed to the guns merely to get the numbers up. Such days are wantonly excessive and do shooting no favours. A good day, with a sensible-sized bag in which everyone has had some memorable shots, and where the birds are all eaten, is, however, justified. The killing of rare birds of prey to safeguard young, reared poults on shooting estates is also not acceptable as their lack of numbers warrants protection. The key, as ever, is about finding the right balance.

With regard to deer and vermin control, there is understandably strict legislation around firearms. Deer Management qualifications are also expected to be held by deer stalkers; these teach participants aspects as varied as shooting accuracy, humane killing, identification, behaviours, close seasons, number management, ecology, biodiversity, gestation periods, reproduction, diseases, meat handling and food hygiene. What it isn't all about is a load of thugs baying for blood. It is in general a well-regulated industry teaching good practice and as much as possible to minimise any suffering by ensuring a humane kill. Such practices are not, for example, adhered to as strongly elsewhere. Personally I don't agree with bow hunting, for example. Thankfully banned in this country, more often than not this type of hunting merely injures the animal, allowing it to run off and die a prolonged, slow and painful death or until it is finished off with an accurate shot from a suitably high-powered rifle.

On the specifics of fox-hunting, in the late spring of 2008 I had the pleasure of sitting next to Lord Bernard Donoghue, at the annual jump-racing awards dinner. Though he is an ex-Labour MP, he sits on racing boards and is a passionate advocate for country sports. He correctly described the fox-hunting ban as a technical loss but a practical win. The numbers now participating in the sport have grown hugely, which I see as a public show of support. Following the huge debate that the subject of fox-hunting has generated, and once they have experienced one of the most traditional and iconic sights of our green and pleasant land, people have been won over by the downright common sense, normality and decency of the people who take part in it.

To conclude, in terms of those now participating, shooting has gone through the roof. No longer is it seen as purely an elitist sport, but one that provides a legitimate and growing revenue for an otherwise underrepresented rural and farming community, and also as a fantastic, ethical and healthy alternative to mass food production.

So back to *Chart Throb* – the prince was laughed at and ridiculed for 'talking to vegetables' twenty years ago, but he was merely championing organic farming, which is now, of course, huge and widely accepted. If the news is to be believed the biggest issues our world now faces are climate change, controlling carbon emissions and developing renewable energy sources. The Prince of Wales was voted number one conservationist by *The Field* and is widely regarded as such, lobbies governments and industries on commercial and community responsibility, and has the moral courage to speak his mind regardless of the effects on his popularity. It is easier to take the route that brings acceptance and popularity, but in the long run such people are the ones who really make a difference. Well, in the end HRH won – whether by cajoling, manipulation or otherwise, eventually the public saw the light.

Chapter 17

Rugby – Then, Now and in the Future

W HEN DESCRIBING THE NATURE of top-level rugby, it is most
easily separated into three different aspects – the culture,
on-field performance and off-field preparation.

First, the culture. 'Rugger' is often perceived as a game for the
upper or middle classes, played on the fields of public schools and
in the cloistered surroundings of Oxford and Cambridge, and
celebrated by the infamous cucumber sandwich brigade of
Twickenham's west car park. In England, this certainly has an
element of truth to it. The Varsity match back in the day, played
by gentlemen with scarves, blazers and pipes, was in fact the
unofficial England trial. It has often been regarded as a thugs'
game played by gentlemen whereas football, or 'association rules'
as it was described at redbrick universities, was in fact the
opposite. This may have been the case in the leafy Home Counties
or the clubs of St James's, but from the turn of the nineteenth
century in the more industrial and farming areas rugby was always
seen as a man's sport. In contrast with the overpaid Italian centre

forward who would feign death, pestilence, famine and torture at the tap of his shin, your West Country farmer, Welsh miner or Yorkshire labourer would gladly lose limbs, chunks of flesh or suffer facial disfigurement in return for a respectful wink or quiet beer after the game.

I see rugby as a brilliant example of how stereotypes have affected and labelled society. The reality is that though football has always been and will always be the more popular sport in England, rugby is synonymous with the community it represents. In New Zealand it is unquestionably the number one sport. Consequently, as the sport of the masses, you inevitably get the odd idiot fan or player trying to make a name for themselves either on or off the field. In Wales too, despite the recent rise in popularity of darts, pool etc., rugby is still seen as the national sport and as such has the broadest range of participants. In England, the majority of state schools play football (it is easier to organise – jumpers for goal-posts, has fewer rules and is easier to understand). Whether it is a status thing or not, the winter term sport for private and grammar schools is most often rugby. However, I would guess that the majority of youngsters who start to play rugby do so through the junior or mini system at local clubs. In my experience, though there may of course be a few rare exceptions, such clubs do an outstanding job, including all the kids who turn up, welcoming newcomers and, in short, providing a focal point for the local community. As a child I remember travelling to Dinas Powys in South Wales and finding the clash of cultures with our lads from affluent South Bucks most entertaining as we basically got beaten up and stuffed 18–5!

Before the game went professional I think it'd be fair to say that rugby was richer for the variety and diversity of the players' backgrounds. Teachers, doctors, lawyers, builders, farmers, miners and policemen, among others, would come together to train a couple of nights a week, exchange a few stories and then crack on on a Saturday afternoon knocking nine bells out of each other and the opposition before drowning themselves in alcohol. In the professional game, though it is sometimes possible to go on to further education, or train in another skill or job, it is increasingly rare and more difficult to do so. This is unfortunately a cultural change in the inevitable nature of professional sport. So asked now if rugby is still an upper-class sport, the answer is unquestionably no.

Access is very good, although perhaps more through local clubs than schools, and to my knowledge it has historically been one of the most welcoming and diverse sports in the country. It has been described as the ultimate team sport. Perhaps this is because (a) no one cares where you're from, what you've done or who you are off the pitch, but simply judges you by your actions on it; (b) rugby is a game in which, like so many other sports, your character is on display more than your personality – there is no faking it and therefore, by being part of a team, you soon develop a special bond, knowing each other more intimately than you would perhaps in any other job except that of the armed forces; and (c) there is a place for everyone, no matter what their size or shape – the lanky ones play lock, the clever ones at halfback, the skinny, quick ones on the wing and the 'fatties' in the front row!

On a professional basis, rugby, like society itself, is becoming more strident and lacking in any sense of personal humility or modesty; it is now seen as a legitimate way of making good money and developing your 'profile', and is increasingly moving main-stream with the notion of celebrity. When I started, rugby wasn't professional and was played purely out of enjoyment by a select few who saw it as a welcome break from the daily grind. Now many of the young lads coming into the professional sport see it as a way to attain fame and wealth.

It would be very easy to become judgemental and harsh about such issues, but it is merely the nature of the sport's growth. Until now, rugby has been somewhat sheltered from the prying eyes of newspapers and glossy magazines. The majority of players have found the stimulation, audience and profile they require by staying within the relatively safe confines of Middle England. Yet the allegation of a sex scandal involving touring England players in Auckland in June 2008, the increasing attention being paid to players' private lives, and, most significantly, the new players' desire to be part of the culture of celebrity, and the benefits it can bring, mean that we're moving closer to mainstream cultures and to that of top-level football.

After the 2003 World Cup, the options open to the likes of Wilkinson, Johnson and others were endless, but, being the characters they are, they modestly decided to stick to the brands already associated with the sport and not do anything that would compromise their dignity and integrity as rugby players. Since then, the Hensons, Dawsons, Brackens, Logans, Ciprianis and Haskells of this world have actively pursued more mainstream and pop-culture opportunities. Again, though it may not be seen as the norm, if it isn't offending anyone and it pays well, then why not go for it? I for one have very little understanding of celebrity-fuelled industries such as gossip magazines, but on brief encounters with them have always been amazed at how contrived and manipulative they all are. It seems that the biggest names in rugby going forward will not merely be the best players, but they will also be the most marketable and – perhaps a note of cynicism here – have the best PR management.

Second, on-field performance. The future of the game will be determined by the demands placed on it. I believe that, on a domestic level, the calibre, intensity and enthusiasm of perform-ance shown during the Guinness Premiership and Heineken Cup in the 2007–8 season illustrated, firstly, how competitive the state of top-end professional rugby in the northern hemisphere is, and, secondly, and more significantly, how far we have come from the relatively stagnant days of early professionalism. Having watched the 1997 All Blacks – arguably the most complete side in rugby history – and then toured New Zealand in 1998, it was clear that, at the advent of professionalism in Great Britain, the distance between the northern and southern hemispheres was more than just a long plane journey. With better weather, an open-air lifestyle and having somehow managed to avoid the dreaded scourge of 'percentage' rugby, New Zealand exuded athleticism, a high level of skill and razzle-dazzle. In contrast, professional rugby here was epitomised by its coarse, almost hobbyist following, beer bellies, outdated stadia, quagmire pitches and, if anyone did have cheer-leaders, they were more tabbing, tattooed roly-polies than the leggy glamour goddesses of the Super 12. With England and France since appearing in three World Cup finals between them, the economies of both countries providing the financial base to support a growing sport and, of course, the realisation and conviction that they could learn from the southern hemisphere and ultimately surpass it, arguably the tide has turned and professional rugby in the northern hemisphere is now in increasingly fine fettle.

Most clubs, having rebranded themselves off the field with more marketable team names – Leicester Tigers, Sale Sharks, Worcester Warriors etc. – have all realised that to pay bills, fill seats and ultimately win things in a climate that is renowned for its fickleness they need to be able to produce an all-court game on it. The games played on hard pitches at the start and end of the season are in general fast-moving, dynamic, vibrant affairs. Between October and March, when the long studs come out and no one wears shorts to training, the games are more tactical and strategic. (I've a theory that you can always tell how the game is going to go by how many layers Paul Sackey turns up in.) Therefore, with demands to play both styles, having the benefit of being a young professional sport and learning from the best and worst practices of other sports – and indeed with a few choice, high-quality imports from foreign pastures to enrich our playing gene pool (not to mention the constant threat of relegation each year) – in my opinion the Premiership has now turned into the best finishing school for complete players. But we shouldn't get too complacent. Many areas have still to be addressed and improved upon, but as an all-round aesthetic product, embracing the new layman, non-anorak supporter, yet still maintaining the balance with the purist's desire for competitive scrums, mauls, pile-ups and the dark arts that only past players can understand, it'd be fair to say that rugby has come a long way since 1998. Who knows, we may even start getting some proper cheerleaders too!

As mentioned before in this book, crowds are also on the increase, with the majority of clubs looking for bigger home venues. Contrast this with the now under-attended Super 14 competition. For a while I was a fan of ring-fencing the Premiership temporarily for the commercial development of the clubs; however, with no threat of losing your job at the end of the season and without the drama that the threat of bailiffs repossessing your house can bring, the effect of eradicating relegation in some ways can be illustrated by the Super 14. Whether it's the fact that your team isn't really playing for anything if it's not in the hunt for the title, or the effect of the new supposedly 'visually enticing' ELVs (experimental law variations), the attendances at 2007–8's Super 14 have been nothing short of dreadful.

So if it's not broken, why fix it? Cue the new ELVs. It is a widely debated new variation on a theme from the International Rugby Board and one especially encouraged by the Australians. The IRB have identified that in some ways speeding up or eradicating the aforementioned dark arts and static parts of the game (scrum, maul, driven lineouts, rucks, tackle area etc.) is the key to spreading the gospel that is rugby football. You should not judge it until you try it, but if you believe that people vote with their feet, then so far the new homogenous basketball-style rugby played under the new laws has not been wholly popular. A few years ago I seriously considered moving to Australia or South Africa to play Super 12 as I loved the pace, skill level and attacking ethos the game embodied. Now, I would pick our stuff every time.

ELVs have currently been out too short a time for me to fully pass judgement but my first impressions are most definitely bad. Very bad. The idea was to make the game more open, fluid and aesthetically pleasing to the non-rugby purist. The reality is that now, as teams can't secure their own ball at the breakdown, each and every breakdown is a complete lottery as to who wins it. As such, no team is willing to run the ball from its own half and risk losing precious territory, and the result is a dull game of ping-pong until one side makes a mistake, at which point the team will camp in the opposition half until it comes away with points, be it three, five or seven or, worse still, give away another penalty in which case you're back to ping-pong again! As I said earlier, people vote with their feet, and it's no coincidence that the 2007–8 Super 14 was the worst attended yet, with the new homogenised format providing less tension, tactical variation and, of course, ball in hand than it was designed to do. Contrast this with the Heineken Cup and Guinness Premiership in 2007–8 where the standard of rugby from almost every team was intense, physical, creative, fast, dynamic, skilful but most of all fun to watch and play. Teams like Wasps prided themselves on going phase after phase until they scored from all parts of the field. There may perhaps be an argument for blaming the players' skill levels or negative coaching, but with the advent of the ELVs we have been encouraged not to do so as the risk of turning over the ball is too high. How dull!

Cynics may suggest that Australia is keenest to press for the new changes because, in terms of pure numbers playing the game, it struggles to continually produce the number of front-five forwards needed to compete at the highest level. A more loose, fluid, less stop-start game would favour their production line in their dry rugby states, where the playing fields are hard and fast, as opposed to those in Bonymaen, Kilkee or Invercargill. One should sample the new rules first before passing judgement, but my guess is that if they are not deemed to be entirely desirable, the referees will ref them more in the way they would do international games than our southern cousins might like, and that refs will hopefully provide clarity at the breakdown as they did before.

In the early nineties, players got themselves as big and strong as possible. The game rarely went beyond three phases and you were left with huge men, big ball carriers willing to crash through walls and grapple bears in the tight five. Simon Shaw, still technically the heaviest man ever to play for England at 130kg, but with an eventful Bristol nightlife weighed considerably more than that, is in contrast now a slender, toned 120kg. The game now demands an awful lot more. Some clubs will regularly go into double figures for phases. The ball is in play for, on average, ten minutes longer in every match and the new ELVs, if they stay, will continue this trend.

When Clive Woodward took the helm, the buzzword was 'versatility'. On the pitch players now had to be all-singing, all-dancing – complete footballers and athletes. Each prop was expected to be able to throw twenty-yard spin passes, backs were expected to ruck and maul and after the first phase the number on your back didn't matter as everyone could switch roles. This was effective to an extent and indeed it must be every coach's wish to have talented athletes who are also intelligent ball players. This has always been the hallmark of a great player and in fact some say that New Zealand earned their name the 'All Blacks' as a modification from the name 'All Backs' from their very first tour of the UK as long ago as 1905–6, alluding to the whole squad's ability to run, pass, kick and score. Yet towards the end of Clive's period in charge he became increasingly set on picking 'specialists'. After all, you might be the most talented prop in the world, but if you can't scrummage then you're not much use. Warren Gatland once told Phil Greening, the effervescent and charismatic hooker, 'Mate, if you spent as much time clearing rucks as you do practising your drop goals I'd pick you over Trevor Leota.'

Looking at that most professional of all sports, the NFL, it seems that the future certainly lies in specialisation: knowing your job, doing it better than your opposite number and being part of the finished jigsaw that makes for a perfect team performance.

Observing Shaun Edwards, although he clearly wants to improve each and every player he works with, he is also a huge advocate of the principle of encouraging players first and foremost to play to their strengths. Inevitably he has come up with a few classic comments along the way: 'Bracks [Peter Bracken, prop] . . . Hey, kid . . . I'm not being funny, but if you touch the ball, something's gone wrong, just clear rucks!'

Another, and one of my all-time favourite quotes from him:

'We won seventeen trophies at Wigan, and we had a move, it was our best move . . . it was called . . . "Give it Kev!" We gave it Kevin Iro, he scored, we won, he got paid, we got paid, everyone's happy. I've got a new one . . . "Give it Oogie"!'

Simple instructions, but unquestionably they work as players then know their role and focus accordingly so as to perform that task to the best of their ability. In addition, if you give simple instructions that can be accomplished and can be measured, rightly or wrongly a player's performance can be thoroughly analysed rather than being left to subjective opinion. Returning to the comparison with American football, there they pick supreme athletes and teach them the rudiments of their jobs. The linebackers are paid to block. The running backs do just that, and the kicker . . . well, you get the picture. This is an overly simplistic comparison when you consider the variety of positions, both in attack and defence, that you will find yourself in during a rugby match, but as the players and coaches become more accountable in the professional age, each person's responsibilities will become more defined. In NFL, the main thinking and decision-making process is laid solely at the door of the quarter back and offensive coach. In rugby, there is already evidence to suggest that, set pieces aside, any such play calling or tactical decisions are only made by the 9, 10 and 12 and on occasions possibly 15. In layman's terms by the 'piano players' as opposed to the 'piano shifters'.

In my experience players welcome direction, provided that they trust and respect the source that it's coming from.

There are, though, few things duller than being part of a team that is contrived and predictable. Having creative inside backs that can work to the team's or coach's grand plan, but within that have the flamboyance to play what's in front of them, react on the hoof and make accurate decisions, is the basis of an exciting and fun team. This moves us neatly on to the aspect of decision-making and leadership, the off-field preparation.

Although I'll be teased for making such an analogy, the decision-making hierarchy in the armed forces bears comparison with that of some of the most successful teams in the sporting field. Let's face it, war has been around a lot longer than professional sport and through trial and error, success and failure, a system has evolved that by and large is extremely effective in getting the best out of the men on the ground.

A senior officer will send out a mission statement as to what the unit under his control is expected to achieve. 'Your mission is to take position X etc.' 'These are your resources ... these are your obstacles: enemy, terrain etc.' What the senior commander will not do is tell the junior commander on the ground how best to carry out the mission. Years of trial and error (think First World War for one!) have taught that the best men to determine how best to achieve the mission are actually those on the ground carrying the mission out. Hence, a culture of leadership has developed that starts with directing the entire army down to commanding section level. Sport can be viewed in a similar way. Away from physically and mentally preparing a side off the pitch, a coach will provide a basic game plan, a structure or format relating to how he sees the best way to beat the opposition. However, once on the field, the players need to take ownership and call, to decide and direct accordingly to achieve the desired success. Quite often the game plan goes out of the window if you feel that another pattern is working, or that a change in tactics is called for – army interpretation: 'The best laid plans never survive first contact' – and so one of the most important and overlooked components is the ability to have good on-field leadership.

All the best rugby teams are player-led. Always have been and always will be. Teams that have success have, in general, evolved over a period together. To name a few, the England team in 2003, the Bath side of the eighties, the 1997 All Blacks and, lastly, the Wasps and Munster sides from 2003 to 2008. People look at individual players and rightly praise their many talents, but these settled sides all had a natural rank structure and hierarchy. Aside from the driven, dynamic culture of ownership the players created, when there was a moment of pressure during a game it wasn't met with a cacophony of shouting and screaming, but a cool, calculated call by the 9 or 10 that everyone bought into and so performed accordingly.

Since the advent of professional rugby, many coaches, being driven, passionate and hard-working, and now with more time to devote to the game, have unintentionally allowed their enthusiasm to become suffocating in the process – 'if this happens we go to move B' . . . 'on the fifth phase of play you two run here' – thus in effect over-coaching. The ideal, once again, is a delicate balance between on-field decision-making, providing player ownership and astute direction or coaching off it. It is true to say that, post-2003, the England setup did not consistently achieve this balance. That's not to lay the blame solely at the feet of the coaches and management, merely to acknowledge that between them and the players there were shortcomings. Ian McGeechan is one man who has always been particularly good at getting the balance right. You'll recall from an earlier chapter that under his management Martin Johnson became captain of the successful 1997 Lions. In late 2008, Martin asked us, the players, to do a presentation to the coaches as to what we required and expected from them. In the past, players turning up at England camp would often be subjected to a couple of days of generic rugby training, even in a test week. This seems unnecessary as surely the rudimentary skills of playing the game are what we do week in, week out at our clubs and, frankly, if we can't catch and pass the ball at this stage we shouldn't be there in the first place. Consequently after canvassing players' views, it was felt that when we were together we shouldn't waste time doing what we did 24/7 back at our clubs. When we were together we should spend what time we had establishing, understanding and practising a clear and concise game plan of what we were to do come Saturday. To that end, the best way to establish on-field leadership and ownership after announcing selection is to have the key decision-makers plan training with the coaches. There is no point in trying to play a game the attack coach wants if 10 and 12 don't believe in it. If the players are involved, a culture of accountability and responsibility is then established. If they have been part of the design process and yet still not performed, then there are no excuses and no one else is to blame but them!

So what of the decision-makers themselves? We've touched on the structure of leadership and how to create a culture of ownership, but if the choices and decisions made aren't good then you're not going to win a raffle let alone trophies.

This to my mind is a potentially huge area for development. I spoke before about the similarity between successful sides, with their on field, player-led decision making ability, and the leadership culture within all military ranks. It is therefore useful to note the comparative lack of specific training that rugby players get in this area. It's interesting that the military invests a lot in the specific development of leadership skills among the junior commanders on the ground, which enables the doctrine of mission command to be implemented successfully. Can you expect to get the same success and authority on the rugby pitch if you don't develop the leadership skills? Surely it is worth investing time and resources in producing more Johnsons and Dallaglios, rather than leaving their creation to pure chance?

With two evenly matched teams, apart from the odd individual mistake, accuracy of execution or stroke of genius that can separate them, it is the tactical decisions that will determine the game's result. To that end, name all the great 9s and 10s to have played the game? What constitutes a great 9 or 10? Is it their ability to run the hundred in sub-eleven seconds, the tricks they can conjure up with the ball or their decision-making ability to correctly manage a game and lead the players around them?

It is important to distinguish between playing ability in terms of the physical and skill elements and the decision-making and control aspects that are the most important requirements of those positions. Carlos Spencer would excite, enthuse and exhilarate, having all the bells and whistles in terms of skills and athleticism. But if you wanted a tactical 10 to control and manage your troops, Andrew Mehrtens would always get the nod. There were more physically capable 10s than Alex King, but in terms of calling the right shots at the right time, in finals his performances as an example of exerting pressure rugby were exemplary. Off the top of my head I can't remember George Gregan or Ronan O'Gara losing behind a dominant pack. What all these players and others like them have in common is experience and intelligence. So, instead of merely leaving a nineteen-year-old halfback to make the right decisions and learn through trial and error till he reaches his peak after more than ten years' experience, would it not be a good idea to coach such an area alongside the bench press and contact drills? As an example of this, it'd be fair to say that the experience of Mike Tindall is hugely influential on the young Gloucester backs. Without his calming influence and persuasive suggestions they have on occasions looked rudderless when put under extreme pressure, despite their undoubted ability and potential.

Jonny Wilkinson is, as everyone knows, one of the most diligent, conscientious and humble characters anyone is likely to meet, but along with the hours spent kicking, tackling, concentrating on his fitness etc., he has on occasion, but specifically in the 2008 Six Nations campaign, been criticised for his 'game management' – that is, his decision-making. 'Why did we decide to run the ball here? Why are we driving that lineout there? Why aren't we speeding the game up now?'

The fact is that no one knows absolutely everything about the game and their decisions aren't always correct, but with all the structuring of units training, set piece, defence and attack patterns, quite often the most important aspect of winning or losing is, amazingly, hardly touched on. There was a time when Jonny was never questioned or challenged as to the reasons behind his decisions and calls when he was playing for England, and it may be that no one challenges or probes him at Newcastle. We all need feedback and without constructive feedback there is a limit to how much we can develop and learn just by ourselves. It seems somewhat unfair to immediately compare him to young Dan Cipriani at Wasps. However, if he or Eoin Reddin make a bad call, not only do they get an earful from other players, but the coaches will also flag it up, and in no uncertain terms. What's more, two bad games in a row and, no matter who you are, you know you're dropped. Consequently, in an exceptionally short period of time such players have developed into astute tacticians, old heads on comparatively young shoulders.

It seems that things such as decision-making ability used to come more naturally than they do now. Before professionalism, with the stimulus of a 'proper' job, working in the real world nine to five, or with the diversity that various life experiences can teach, players would in general be less sheltered and would not rely as much on the coaches for direction. Therefore, as the modern professional becomes increasingly spoon-fed and the preparation element of the game develops, the areas of decision-making and leadership will become increasingly emphasised. The best organisations are already doing work in this area with the ever-proficient Eddie Jones recruiting the skills of Michael Lynagh to work with the Saracens academy. But if you can in some way impart some of the knowledge and experience of the Jonathan Davieses, Lynaghs, Kings, Dean Richardses, O'Garas, Gregans or Sean Fitzpatricks of this world into a young man's head, then surely that's an investment worth making that may perhaps make them peak earlier, at twenty-two, rather than at twenty-eight or twenty-nine?

Chapter 18

What Next?

I T IS AN INTERESTING FACT that we are only just beginning to see the coming to maturity of players who have only ever known the professional game. As I have already said, when I started playing top-level rugby the game was indeed professional, but it was mostly played by those who retained a modicum of reality, outside interests or another trade. I've always tried to work hard to develop and maintain interests and possibilities outside the game, but we are entering a time in which some players leaving the game have never done a day's work outside that of being a professional sportsman. Inevitably some will have 'made it' and their names will be enough for them to enter the realms of punditry and journalism; or, for the superstars, as a face or a recognised personality, opportunities will arise in the media or celebrity circus. Yet these opportunities are limited and even the number of positions open to players moving directly into coaching is capped. This is a challenge that the professional game in this country will have to face, something that the Professional Rugby Players' Association (the body that looks after the welfare of professional players) is rightly and energetically addressing. But you can only lead a horse to water. To that end, the PRA provides a comprehensive range of work placement opportunities, training and contacts for the players to follow; however, it seems that so far the players currently keenest to exercise such possibilities are those who are the least likely to need the help.

You don't enter the big wide world of work after following pretty much the same routine for twelve years without a certain amount of trepidation. For me personally, although I'm lucky enough to have had a few options and possibilities open to me, knowing that the next career is likely to encompass starting a family, establishing 'home' and seeing me through to retirement means that the decisions I make can be quite forbidding, even daunting. It isn't just amongst fellow sportsmen, however: I find it a very common trait among thirty-something adults in this country. Most have had ten-odd years' working experience, have established who they are, what they enjoy, what their interests are and, in a work environment, what their relative strengths and weaknesses are. After leaving school or university, for the majority it has been a case of falling into something that works and pays, their twenties then being a series of opportunities in which they've attempted to establish themselves in a particular trade or industry. However, when they hit an age when they have to start considering where they want to be, where their life is going, and so on, then with this knowledge, experience and the options before them, they realise that the next decision they make will probably be the big one.

The army loses a huge amount of ability around mid to senior captain level. Young officers, having done a few operational tours, been in a dynamic, challenging environment, developing themselves from young men and women into capable adults, and having enjoyed some great life experiences, not to mention a few Uncle-Albert-during-the-war stories arising from the current conflicts, leave for a more settled lifestyle. After a period of operational command, and quite often faced with a period of desk work and at a time when many look to settle down, with the possibility of earning City money, many then opt for civvie street. The problem is that, being the driven characters they are, many then miss the adrenalin, challenge and excitement that life once provided; no matter how much you earn or who you go home to, the overhead blast of a 50 cal. or an RPG just can't be the same as equating a balance sheet at Wernham Hogg with David Brent and Co!

Playing sport is perhaps the same. Once you've left you may have more time to plan your social life, earn more money or go on to do amazingly well, but can you replace the feeling you get before a final at Twickenham? The nerves during the week, the sick feeling you get boarding the coach, the range of emotions in the dressing room or when you sing the anthems? The anticipation of a million eyes waiting for the ball to come down from the heavens or, best of all, the exhausted, contemplative satisfaction after the event – the body battered, floating on a wave of endorphins, the mind euphoric, knowing that you delivered when it mattered most? I retired from playing professional rugby at the end of the 2008/09 season and so these are questions I now ask myself. I had in fact originally planned to retire at the end of the previous season, but the lure of emulating the 1997 Lions and having more success than in 2005, as well as encouragement from a couple of close friends persuaded me to stay. Sadly, I didn't achieve my goal of playing for the Lions and it was also a disappointing year on the field at Wasps, where I'd decided to concentrate my efforts after retiring from international rugby. Was it therefore a bad decision? Well for the first time in years, I was fully involved in all aspects of the club. I wasn't constantly away on various England training sessions, which allowed me to spend more time with the other lads and really get to know them. For the first time I also had the luxury of being able to go for a coffee or bite to eat after training, rather than having to rush to some sponsor engagement, community scheme, charity event or media request. As a result my quality of life improved and I was getting more enjoyment out of playing for the club and felt that I really belonged there. When I played my final game at Adams Park, I hadn't for one second thought I would become emotional. But when the lads made me run out first to a standing ovation, the thoughts of what we'd put in, what we'd all shared through the years and what we'd achieved whilst wearing that shirt simply overwhelmed me. I told the crowd afterwards, 'You only realise what you've got when you've got to let it go'. Some things are more important than trophies.

It may be quite sad to say so, but, put simply, I just love the game. There were times when the issues and politics that accompany the playing of it professionally angered or frustrated me, but in its purest form I always did and always will get a lot of enjoyment out of rugby. In the off-season, I'll still wander along to Clapham Common or Richmond and join random punters throwing a ball around. There's a developmental aspect to it for me in terms of the carefree stimulus and freedom of decision-making I get from it, but essentially it just reminds me why I played the game in the first place. To that end I knew we'd found the right place when, within five minutes of arriving in St Agnes (Cornwall) and I was in our house unpacking, there was a knock on the front door.

Eight ten- to twelve-year-olds stood there, looking a little sheepish.

'Arwright, Josh ... Coming out to play?'

'I'm in my thirties! ... All right then, I'll get my boots.'

No doubt I'll always enjoy throwing a ball around in the park but, playing wise, I wanted to go out on my terms, at the top. What I did not want to do was play on indefinitely, dropping level after level as the arthritic joints stiffen and the hamstrings shorten.

Having had rugby dominate my entire life I'm most excited about the next step. The world is a big place with rugby being, in real terms, a fairly insignificant part of it. With lots of things to see, do and achieve out there I think it'd be fair to say that it's been a tick in the box for rugby, so what's next?

I'd love one day to have a family and provide a loving home for my wife and children, but, before that happens and before proper responsibilities come along, I want to make the most of the opportunities available. As such, I fancy a challenge and an adventure – something on which, when I'm old and grey, I can look back fondly and think that I made the most of my time. As I explained in Chapter 15, my good friend Keith Reesby and I trekked up the Baltoro Glacier a few summers back, to K2. It was our summer off and supposedly a 'holiday'. It was, of course, fairly minging, eating predominantly goat soup for three weeks having done precisely no training for it whatsoever. Though we didn't mention it at the time, it was, in fact a trial, or 'recce', to see how we would get on together in such an environment. Despite Keith having a slight sense of humour failure at me encouraging our guide to carry his weight for him (as an army lad it is the ultimate insult to have someone else carry your weight for you, especially when the guide is in his sixties!) and me spilling my pee pot inside my sleeping bag at 3 a.m. because I wouldn't get out of it to take one (it was minus-20 outside) it was relatively harmonious. Therefore we've planned something bigger and better: we're aiming to climb Everest in May 2010 and we started training in the summer of 2009. Our preparation has included spending ten days in the Bavarian Alps, various weekends away climbing during the winter and then also a full dress rehearsal on Aconcagua, the 7,000-metre Andean peak, which is the highest outside of the Himalayas. It's also very cold! My plan for after Everest is to start working as a management consultant for PricewaterhouseCoopers and so as well as spending time working towards the Everest expedition, I will also spend some of the year in the office, learning about the business and working on various projects. This means that when I come back and start full-time, I can hit the ground running and not be shaking hands for the first time. I don't want to go straight into the job – I have a final itch to scratch and, for me, Everest is that itch and will be the ultimate challenge to face before getting to grips with real life and proper responsibilities.

I was drawn to management consultancy partly because of my background in sport. I'm fascinated by leadership in all its guises and the dynamics between people in a professional context, but more significantly I'm interested in the differences between a successful and unsuccessful environment – between winning and losing. I'll be drawing on my experiences in sport, the army and the various other enterprises I've been part of over the years but most of all I'm looking forward to learning something new. Whatever job we choose, we seem to base the decision on a combination of three factors – fulfilment, lifestyle and of course, rather unfortunately, the need for money. For me, management consultancy seems (for the moment at least) to have the best balance of these, in line with my areas of interest. In addition, aside from the mental stimulation, it appears – from the outside at least – that the key challenge is to add genuine value and really make a lasting difference on worthwhile, tangible projects. I know I left professional rugby early but I want to learn something new, as I know that for some time, I haven't fully utilised my potential. There were of course attractive offers to continue playing, which came from various UK clubs, as well as from France and even Australia. These foreign offers I found more tempting as working abroad is something I would have liked to have experienced. But despite the short term rewards and luxury on offer, I'd set my goals and decided to stick to them.

I was very sorry not to be selected for the 2009 Lions tour to South Africa. I would have loved to have gone, knowing that it is probably the best place to tour, but also that the coaching staff selected would strike the right balance between when to switch on and work and when to have fun and enjoy. It is very difficult talking about issues that have meant so much to me and that haven't gone my way, for fear of coming across as bitter or negative. What I will say is that it was clear that Wasps had a fairly disappointing year and that didn't do my cause any favours in terms of selection, especially as I wasn't playing on the international stage. Without mentioning the conversations that led to my decision to leave international rugby, I ultimately felt somewhat let down and used by people I thought I could trust. No hard feelings there but it was a revealing moment that hopefully I can learn from later in life. The time it hurt most was while watching the first test and seeing the Lions crossing the line unsuccessfully three times, and as in the 2007 World Cup final, whether correct or otherwise, I felt that, hand on heart, I could have made a difference to the result. Alas, I guess some things just aren't meant to be.

A very good friend of mine at Sandhurst was once put under pressure when selecting the sergeants' cadre (the annual selection of the very best NCOs in the British Army). At the time the army was desperate to recruit more women and my friend was told that, given an equal choice between a man and a woman, he should opt for a woman because politically it was more acceptable. That's fine, but what if it's not 50/50? He suggested to his colonel that if they ever opened the floodgates as a result of such politically correct pressure and representation by numbers, rather than purely on quality alone, then the entire selection process would have its integrity undermined as every other member selected (or not selected) would know the injustice and go back to their individual units with just a little bit less faith in the system. He wasn't willing to compromise, and offered his badge rather than put his name to the paper. He knows who he is, and I admire him enormously for it. Perhaps his sentiments are out of date and archaic, but such values are the hallmarks of trust and honesty in any occupation.

Although the international game obviously attracts huge attention each year, those who follow the Guinness Premiership or Heineken Cup will be familiar with the general high standard, extremely competitive nature and all-round excellent entertainment that the clubs now produce. It can be legitimately argued that at its best club rugby is often at a higher standard than the international game. Being part of a challenging but ultimately winning environment is not always the easiest thing, but it is certainly the most rewarding.

What some who haven't been there can fail to appreciate is how much extra commitment is part and parcel of being involved with the international game. There is, of course, the extra time away from home. This may sound ridiculous, but, especially for the guys with families, it is a huge commitment to leave your loved ones for long periods of time. I distinctly remember the look on Simon Shaw's face when, having just got back from four days away with the club on a European game to drop his bags at home, he saw the elation in his daughter's eyes turn to tears as he walked back out through the door, leaving immediately for a week of holding tackle bags in yet another mediocre England camp.

In addition, there are commitments to sponsors. One can hide away from the attention to some extent at club level, but do something amazing in the white shirt and charity requests flood in, the press want interviews and the sponsors queue up demanding appearances. This is not to be knocked; it is part and parcel of playing a professional sport and, not least, a way of making money. However, if your main motivation isn't purely to raise your profile or earn money, then if it isn't fundamentally enjoyable for any of the reasons expressed above and you genuinely believe that your club is a better-run organisation than the international setup, it can be better being back at the club. It is the Alan Shearer or Roy Keane scenario. The clubs have also become aware of this and, despite the new six-year agreement between the RFU and the professional clubs that sets out the control, accessibility and availability of the players, a player is still better value to them if he doesn't leave to play international rugby and, as such, they are increasingly offering financial incentives to players not to do so.

I, as any rugby fan, just want England to win. Whether or not I'm involved, I hate seeing them lose and, worse still, if I'm ever in a bar or pub watching a game I feel genuine embarrassment and shame if the supporters feel let down by the performance. The alarming aspect is that, with such rich resources and with so many positive aspects to the English game, the performance isn't hard to put right. There is so much to be excited about English rugby at the moment. Most of the clubs have predominantly English players, and in most positions three or four players could probably quite comfortably slip on the international jersey and excel. The clubs are increasingly seeing larger and larger crowds, and most are looking for bigger stadiums. The quality of the rugby being played at the top end of the Premiership and in the Heineken Cup is every bit as good as, and in some cases better than, international rugby, and, lastly, England's most successful captain of all time is finally at the helm of the national team. I may be looking a bit too far ahead, but with the six-year agreement with the clubs in place and any potential accountability or excuses being eradicated we could well be at the dawn of great new age for the English game.

I've met some fantastic people during my rugby career. Some make you laugh, others make you reflect or just entertain you, but occasionally you meet someone who not only impresses you but stands out as an influence on you, whether directly or indirectly. The first, of course, was Richard Rivett; the next was Shaun Edwards.

With a plethora of trophies both as a player and now as a coach, Shaun Edwards is widely regarded as one of the best coaches around. People are always fascinated about what it's like behind the scenes – what such and such a person is like or some revealing stories. However, as a recent convert to rugby union, Shaun's reputation in rugby league has preceded his success in union and as a result the spotlight is increasingly falling on this complex but brilliant man. It is difficult when writing a book to describe with absolute objectivity what someone is like, particularly when you are so close to them, and I hope that the following will be taken in the spirit of affection in which it is intended.

Shaun is, in short, completely mad. The players love him for it. His eccentric dress sense, the schizophrenic tendencies, the larger than life, restless character and his intrinsic kindness to all he meets. I would want no other coach in the world on my side, but on occasions I know that I've wanted to throttle him. He cares so much about what he does. He fears failure and will stop at nothing to achieve results. The beauty about him and the reason players respect him comes from his complete lack of ego. He cares first, second and third about the rugby, not his position or status but being as good as he can be, and he draws enjoyment and satisfaction accordingly. If that means upsetting the system he is willing to do so. His boundless energy is infectious, although somewhat exhausting, and he is one of the most competitive people I've ever met.

Looking at his past you can pick out the various character traits. His father was reputedly very much from the 'tough love' school, wanting the best for his boy but driving him single-mindedly, intolerant of failure. The pair are alleged to have had a fist fight during a schools international above the advertising hoardings at Headingley! Sources from his rugby league days suggest how much he has been influenced by black culture. Having grown up next to Ellery Hanley and Martin Offiah, he admired most in others the one element that he perhaps lacked himself – natural athleticism. I find this staggering, for as a player he was intelligent, a fierce competitor and a phenomenal ball player. What he wasn't was a ball carrier who could win a game single-handed, or a world-renowned finisher with a nickname 'Chariots'. He has always had relationships with beautiful athletic black women and cites Grace Jones as the ultimate woman. Even now, when selecting players to join the club, where most will look for innate footballing talent and intelligence, Shaun's first instinct is, like an NFL scout, to look for genetics – general, natural sporting ability – he'll spend hours attempting to develop the footballing bit afterwards.

Though he enjoys the buzz of the public arena and the interaction with others, like all natural competitors he is more often, I would wager, a loner, consumed by his own thoughts. You'll often see him reading a book before a game or at half-time. These aren't his notes, or coaching hints. They are novels, poetry or religious texts – anything to soothe his mind, to distract him from the noises and voices within.

We all revel in the contradictions and ironies of his actions. One time we had an audience with the late Pope John Paul II. On the bus leaving the Vatican, everyone silent in contemplative mood, Shaun interrupted his prayer as his mobile rang out:

'Oh, 'ello mate, that's right, 14.30 Lingfield, three hundred on the nose, cheers, pal.'

Religion has played a huge part in his life and, especially since losing his brother, it provides a source of peace, harmony and perspective for his otherwise restless mind.

In terms of management style, he would be your classic regimental sergeant major. He is the heartbeat of the club, the driving force and energy behind the motivation and morale of the men. The men would die for him, being both protective and loyal but eager to impress: a word of praise or respect from Shaun means something and can lift your entire day. However, there is a fine line between being the driver, being hands-on and making things happen, and being a tyrant or a dictator. It is a delicate balance knowing when to step back and allow ownership for those below you. There are times when he's wrong or the players or indeed other coaches disagree with him. It takes a strong character to stand firm against such a strong will and on occasions he and I have come close to blows. On such occasions you need to step back to be able to see the bigger picture and as such every RSM needs his general to give vision or strategy to the big picture. His all-consuming passion and all-embracing character especially suit the aspect of coaching. Though capable in aspects of management as well as leadership (with the added stimulus of Wales, I believe that his coaching was almost impeccable in the 2007–8 season), the role of director of rugby, with its more strategic demands, would not be one he'd enjoy. Without embarrassing him, the good news for Wasps, Wales and the Lions is that he continues to improve. Like all great achievers, he has an insatiable appetite for self-improvement and learning, coveting opinions and trusted advice. He watches more rugby than anyone I know, and he's often first at the club, punishing his body with gruelling fitness sessions in the insalubrious surroundings of Wasps' training ground after a night on the tiles.

Close friends with people from a broad spectrum of society, from shady characters to priests and barristers, he has a particular bond with Steve Collins, the former world champion boxer. As such, along with his obsession with athleticism, like any top fighter he's continually clambering on to the scales to see how many ounces he has gained or lost. One of my fondest memories of him is told by Dave Walder, who was eager to engage his new boss after recently signing for the club.

Shaun had done an hour or so shadow boxing in a packed gym when he disappeared before returning in just his Speedos to climb on to the scales in front of everyone. Swearing freely and obviously unhappy with the result, already sweating and breathing hard, he stripped stark naked so as to lose any extra weight he could. Unsurprisingly, the entire gym had come to a halt by this stage, looking on in sheer disbelief. Still not happy, he moved the scales to another part of the gym, as though the ground on which they were standing would make a difference, and then stormed off again in a huff. I'm reliably informed that he asked to borrow a razor from one of the lads and then proceeded to relinquish his remaining surplus weight (his pubes!) in the bin next to him. He returned one last time, bald turkey intact, for another round of expletives before accepting the fact that he had put on a few pounds and then, thank goodness, put on some clothes!

Being selected for the Lions is the highest accolade a coach or player can aspire to in the British Isles. The reason Shaun was given for his exclusion from the 2005 tour, despite unprecedented club success, was that he hadn't coached internationally. Without mentioning the issues that resulted in him coaching Wales as opposed to the England team, for a player or even a fan to have him involved in the 2009 Lions tour against the world champions was a mouth-watering prospect. Being a collection of 'silverbacks', signs of tenderness or emotion are seldom displayed by these rugby alpha males. But the beauty of sport is that on occasions – in those special moments – it can reveal raw emotions that our normally reserved character keeps under wraps. Who will forget Paul Gascoigne crying at Italia 90, or the demons being banished by Stuart Pearce when he scored that penalty six years on? Derek Redmond being helped around the track in tears by his father, or Darren Clarke in the Ryder Cup after losing his wife? Having been through a hell of a journey for the last seven years with Shaun, with both of us being non-expressive types, just as my emotions overcame me at the end of the World Cup final in 2003 so I'll have no shame in giving that mad, tormented, brilliant man a well-deserved hug on reaching the pinnacle in his career. And what's more, even though the Lions did not emerge triumphant, as I sincerely hoped they would, I trust that somewhere, in a brief respite between euphoria and exhaustion after future successes, which no doubt he will have, he will at least allow a moment to love himself.

People often ask me if the idea of coaching appeals. The answer in short is perhaps one day but definitely not now. Last season I co-coached the Richmond women's team, during which we proudly won the National Cup final by a record margin against the formidable Saracens side. It was a great experience and I learned a lot about the art of coaching and what's more, respect for those who do it! The girls were superb fun, sometimes challenging, sometimes wonderful and of course one or two sometimes a complete pain in the arse. Working with the different characters and personalities, both in terms of the coaching squad and players was very enlightening. I saw it from the other side for the first time and found that if one strikes the correct balance between coaching, managing, and leading it can be hugely rewarding. As I mentioned, I still completely love the game and have some novel ideas on how a team could be run slightly differently, which would be interesting to trial but for the foreseeable future my sights are set elsewhere. As I said earlier, I've always worked hard outside the sport to give myself some options after rugby. So it is both with apprehension and excitement that I look to the future. I have many passions, the military, politics, financial systems, law, management, property, farming, travel among them, and you can even now add writing to that list – or perhaps not! One thing I do know is that I don't want to live off a past reputation. I suppose that, as for everyone else, the challenge is to balance everything – the excitement, the fulfilment of earning money, making a difference, having fun and being a good husband and father.

I deliberately haven't mentioned many aspects of my private life, but Vanessa and I got married in January 2008. At her hen do, one of her best friends explained to her that she hadn't picked the easy option. This is true . . . being beautiful and bright, she could have picked many more suitable and sensible types but, in attempting to sum up the way I try to live my life, I'll quote Richard Branson, 'The brave may not live for ever, but the cautious do not live at all'.

My Greatest XV and Other Legends

1. Christian Califano

No doubt of pure French pedigree, however it could be argued that unlike the houses of Latour, Petrus and Lafite he didn't mature as well. But when in his prime shortly after the advent of professionalism he played for Toulouse, the cornerstone of European rugby, and in the much-revered French pack it could be said that Califano changed and revolutionised his position.

Props have always had a reputation of being somewhat stoic, silent assassins but always formidable scrummagers. Califano had it all. Phenomenal at the set piece but also incredibly mobile, dynamic and the joker of the team to boot.

2. Sean Fitzpatrick

Quite simply, a hero of mine. This may seem bizarre as, playing in the backs, you tend to want to emulate the silky hips, the outright speed or sheer cheek of the glamour boys. However, for rugby purists, or those who know the game, it's in the tactical nuances and mental battles that the big games are won or lost. Fitzpatrick epitomised everything that was wily, cunning, astute and unrelentingly competitive. To note just how few times he came off the field for his understudy Warren Gatland is testament enough. He captained arguably the most complete team in rugby history – the 1997 All Blacks – and despite not lifting a World Cup was credited with the psychological preparation of Jonah Lomu in the 1995 World Cup.

3. Graham Price

You know you've reached greatness when people write songs about you. Part of the phenomenal trio that was the Pontypool front row, this man was carved from the very rock his compatriots in South Wales quarried. From the industrial heartland of farming, steelworks and mining, he came from a place where men of toil and graft needed champions to inspire them and put this little valley town firmly and proudly on the world map. When Graham Price single-handedly destroyed the New Zealand eight to the point that they put just three in the scrum on the 1977 Lions tour, he did just that.

4. Martin Johnson

Outside the political wings of Lansdowne Road's stadium officials, you'd have to travel a long way to find someone who'd have anything too derogatory to say about English rugby's Bobby Moore. Renowned more for his furrowed brow, intimidating persona and temper, these belie an incredibly sharp and bright rugby mind. Not one to waste words, in his early years Johnson had the reputation for being an archetypal 'Leicester mong', but with captaincy came responsibility, on which he thrived. This may be somewhat simplistic, but it is with the front five in general that the game is won or lost; in most cases it is a street fight with a few rules chucked in. For that reason I like big, hard, horrible bastards who are going to give you ball going forward. As with most people, they can be amiable and average or difficult but driven. For most, God gives with one hand and takes away with the other – you can be made of nails and dumb, or skilful and bright but soft. It is a rare treat to be handed all the assets – and the very greatest players tend to have been. Johnno had it all. The only other person I would mention here is a certain Simon Shaw. Although I am perhaps biased, in my opinion he has been the most influential player at Wasps, and thus the Premiership, over the last ten years. Had he been from a different era or played in a different position, his name could be up here instead.

5. John Eales/Willie John McBride

What can you say about a two-times-winning World Cup captain, playing second row, who also takes the goal kicks? John Eales is the kid at school you want to hate but who gives you no reason to do so, who you can't help admiring because he dates the prom queen, who captains the sports teams and is also a genuinely lovely fellow. The other choice is Ireland's favourite son. I've not met Willie John, but there seems to be something consummately human and approachable about him. They say that rugby is a thugs' sport played by gentlemen; well, there are plenty of men I've played with who aren't particularly gentle and I'm sure Willie was no different. However, rugby to me has, rightly or wrongly, always been a sport where your true character is revealed on the field of play and not in the bravado, gesturing and verbal exchanges off it. Huge men who are capable of enormous intimidation and feather ruffling find no need to behave like that. The small man's affliction seldom exists as these giants, capable of such confrontation and physical violence on the field, are content and comfortable in their own skins off it. Willie John McBride typifies that figure for me; this gently spoken, kind, grandfatherly figure, having done it all with nothing left to prove, has a good man's eyes in a warrior's face. He would be a tribal elder now, but when the women were away or had their backs turned, I could imagine him still being one of the boys, whispering a naughty tale or one-liner.

6. Mike 'Iron Mike' Teague

There are many who would, I'm sure, debate this choice. Many would opt for the effervescent and iconic Lawrence Dallaglio, Michael Jones or Francois Pienaar. I didn't really see that much of Jones or, indeed, of Pienaar as he rose to fame in the days of apartheid. Lawrence has obviously been a good teammate and would probably make most people's team, but I've tried where possible not to consider anyone I've been particularly close to. It may seem bizarre, but in training and playing with individuals daily you begin to see them as human beings and not as the mythical figures they seem to others. They obviously have flaws or weaknesses, just as you do, but in many ways, like a small child idolising his heroes, I don't want the reality, I want the dream. Thus I pick 'Iron Mike'. There was a moment in the 1989 Lions tour of Australia when he turned the tide to eventually win the test series. It was not pretty, it did not need much cunning, but it worked, and all's fair in love and war. Having been outplayed in the first test against a superior Australian team it seemed that the writing was on the wall for us. As I've already mentioned, rugby can on occasions be all about pure brutality. When all else has failed can we beat them up? This isn't, of course, an advocation of violence but to pretend that Robert Jones's baiting of Nick Farr-Jones wasn't a cue for or a prelude to the all-out mayhem that followed would just be a lie. Like the famous '99' call (the 'one in, all in' policy for on-pitch violence used in the 1974 Lions tour of

South Africa), or Douglas Jardine's Bodyline tactic, what followed was at its most basic a rutting stag establishing who's really the boss. The ref was never going to send off twenty people in the same game. Of all those scrapping, no one underlined his dominance more than the builder from Gloucester. The point of this tale is not to understate his immense playing ability, but with Steve Tyneman's nose splayed all over Queensland, Australia deep down knew that, though they were better at rugby, in terms of primeval language they were not top dog. The Lions won 2–1 and that's all the history books will say. I just wish we'd done the same in 2005!

7. Richie McCaw

The current New Zealand captain, totem, national hero and, it could be argued, the greatest player of all time. An eloquent ambassador for the sport, skilful, bright and not to mention a good-looking bugger, he is yet another of those kids at school you can't help but feel jealous of. However, selection has been described as an art not a science. You go on feeling and instinct, not statistics. Therefore it is character that matters most. It is character that people follow and are inspired by, not the technicalities of the player. I say this more out of respect than from a desire to gloat, but truly to acquire the title of Greatest Ever, which he obviously has the ability to be, he would need to lift the World Cup and he hasn't done that yet. I was once told that you don't play open-side flanker without having something wrong with you; why else would you opt for being, in effect, a bottle top that doesn't want to be removed? You're at a party and, without the necessary implement, everyone takes turns at chewing, hitting, scraping and gouging, trying to remove you from the thing they really want to get at!

8. Dean Richards

This may seem strange as Dean Richards was for me the antithesis of dynamic, professional rugby, everything I didn't like about the English game. With his socks rolled down, I can honestly not remember him running . . . ever! If I was coaching a team I'd take the educated right foot, footballing gall and sheer audacity of Zinzan Brooke, but being slightly more measured with age, in a World Cup final I'd probably find myself banking on the nous, craft and sheer dogged hardness of Leicester's favourite copper. I played against him on a couple of occasions in my early days at Bristol. I once carried the ball into the ruck, which resulted in what was effectively a human gralloching. I've always considered myself reasonably strong, especially for my size, but his bone-raw strength was like that of a bear ripping the limbs off a lamb. Lastly, why did you never see him run? As the line from Martin Scorsese's *Goodfellas* goes, 'He didn't move too fast, but he was the boss – he didn't have to', clear evidence of a savvy mind – the game came to him.

9. Robert Jones/Rob Howley/George Gregan

I played with the first two, one with Bristol, the other with Wasps. I mentioned above how I preferred not to consider those that I'd played with. However, I was so much younger than Robert Jones at Bristol that he still kept his untouchable tag for me, and Stan (from Laurel and Hardy), as Ron Howley was known, was only at Wasps for one year, during which he hardly ever trained, so basically he's included too. I was once in a bar with two university mates of Welsh descent, with the rest of the Bristol team in there too. Mark Denney introduced them to some of the boys:

'Hi, lads, this is Rob, Rob this is Gareth and Ewan.'

They stood there shocked, knowing full well who it was.

'Oh, but that's Sir Rob to you!'

Robert Jones and George Gregan were for me very similar players. With immaculate distribution, being comparatively small, though capable of it they weren't renowned for their running game but, as with all strategists, they were little generals, the true piano players bossing and controlling the shifters in front of them. I grew up as a huge fan of Robert Jones and, coming from the nearby village to my mother's Cwmllynfell, he was often the talk of the town. George Gregan is one of the greatest players, competitors and ambassadors in the sport. Having been the most capped player in the world of all time, I was amazed and impressed to learn, when we bumped into him on a recent holiday, that at the age of thirty-five he'd agreed to another two-year playing contract in Japan. On questioning him about his decision, if, with all the hits, the body would be able to cope, he succinctly answered in a way that illustrated his wit, brains and cunning: 'Mate, have you seen the way I play?' Lastly, Rob Howley, probably the best overall 9 I've ever seen; a blend of guile, tactical nous and strategic ability, he combined his greyhound-like physique with great athleticism and running ability. What was most fitting was that at the end of an injury-dogged career, and one often spent behind retreating packs, he finally got his just reward in the most climactic endings on the peak of club rugby's Everest – the 2004 Heineken Cup final. It was a privilege to play with him.

10. Jonathan Davies

Let it be said, you can forget about the statistics, the analysis, game plans, intelligence and match-ups: what I fundamentally love about sport is its unknown quantity. To that end, I've always favoured a 10 who has a touch of enigma about him. The most intriguing aspects of life are the unknown ones – God, religion etc. – so putting your faith into something untouchable, something magical, seems fitting for me. Back to Gareth and Ewan. J.D., or

'Jiffy', came up to Bristol with 'Sir Rob' one night. One of the freshers, keen on rugby but not an anorak like the rest of us, recognised the man's stance and familiar face but wasn't quite sure who he was.

'Gar . . . who's that over there?'

'Jonathan.'

'Jonathan who?'

'THERE'S ONLY ONE JONATHAN!'

Like the greats – Carwyn James, Phil Bennett, Barry John – he was educated at the greatest of fly-half factories. As Max Boyce once said, 'Some people think it doesn't exist, but hidden deep in the mines so that rugby league scouts can't find it is the outside half factory.' The reality was that it was a Llanelli grammar school called the Gwendryth. There has always been something magical about the Welsh number 10 shirt, but along with his wizardry Jonathan Davies discovered the drive of a professional from being brought up in a council house without a father. He is the BBC's best rugby commentator; like Michael Johnson on athletics, he is articulate, accurate and, most importantly, strikes the right balance between being fair while still giving his opinion rather than merely sitting on the fence.

As a player he was my favourite. The first book I bought with my own money was called simply *Jonathan*. Bill McLaren's commentary still reverberates in my head now: 'Reverse pass by Jones, out to Davies, he steps off his left, puts the ball past White, searing acceleration . . . OH! . . . he's like will-o'-the-wisp.'

It was my first international I was there. In many ways, as a young fly half I looked to have, or at least liked to think I had, similar traits. Small, quick, cheeky and competitive. It is a shame that rugby union was robbed of one of its best talents as he matured both physically and mentally on his move to league and it is one of my few regrets that he didn't play for the Lions. There is one other player who reminds me of him. There have, of course, been many great 10s – from the mercurial in the sixties and seventies to the machine-like reliability of those in the nineties, through to old Golden Balls himself who banished his own as well as a nation's sense of self-doubt with one sweetly timed kick with his weaker foot. However, without meaning to be too premature, in young Dan Cipriani (of Wasps) I have seen someone who has the potential to be better than all the others. It's easy to want to judge players on one brilliant performance, and not to remain objectively analytical, but I see in him a talent like no other. His abilities are unquestionable, encompassing speed, athleticism and footballing ability, but he, like Jonathan, is also capable of the sublime and delectable. However, to be considered a great 10 you not only have to have ability but also game management and leadership skills. Danny can be an awkward little bugger, fiercely competitive and challenging of those around him. Many people call him arrogant and dismiss him as someone too sure of himself. I don't care about that. Given a choice between a teammate who's a complex and challenging winner or an amiable Mr Nice Guy who won't rock the boat, I'll pick the competitive one every day of the week. Such characters are often perceived as disruptive or difficult. This isn't the case; they just need good, honest, strong management from someone they respect and trust or someone who will channel the ownership of the team through them so as to maintain standards in others. Without such management and guidance, they can be detrimental to a team. But Danny, given the responsibility of playing 10, is the decision-maker and thrives under pressure. When he makes mistakes, his peers and bosses let him know in no uncertain terms that he has done so, but given the reins in a well-managed, constructively critical environment, he will continue to learn and could well become the greatest of all time.

11. Rory Underwood

Most people would go for arguably the biggest name in world rugby history, Jonah Lomu, who was unquestionably a phenomenon in the 1995 World Cup. However, amazing as he was, Jonah was physically so much more advanced than anyone of his day or before him, but that was it. If you could, as the South Africans did, front up to his power, then you could just about keep him under control. In the days of amateurism his sheer athleticism and size bulldozed teams the world over. However, I've not gone for him as, advanced for his day as he was, if he was playing now would he create the same impact? Big and powerful undoubtedly, but the Tuilagis, Bannermans and Tuqiris have similar physiques and thus I'd go for a slighter man, one with a more varied array of weapons. Underwood was a brilliant, brilliant finisher, mentally strong and brave to boot. Being a RAF pilot he is also bright and able, and also a frighteningly nice guy. The closest to him and someone who, to be honest, I would have picked ahead of him is Billy Whizz himself – Jason Robinson. He had all of Rory's attributes, but perhaps also had a more all-round footballing game, playing lots at full back too. For reasons mentioned above, however, I consider Jason too close a colleague to be able to pick him.

12. Tim Horan

To me the centre partnership is about the combination. You need chalk and cheese, hammer and sickle, sweet and sour. Think Tindall and Greenwood, Little and Bunce, Carling and Guscott, Maggs and Waters. Like a good marriage, the strengths of one should complement the other. Too similar to each other and it doesn't work. Pick Gibbs and Bunce and no one's seeing the ball, Guscott and Greenwood and you've got yourself a turnstile. I loved the combination of Scott Gibbs and Jeremy Guscott on the 1997 Lions tour. That tour was not won at the moment the fluid and graceful Guscott dropped the goal, but when, on a bull-like charge, 'Gibbsy' confronted and toppled that symbol of South African manhood, the huge Os du Randt. 'The Ox', talisman of their scrum and the personification of masculinity, was dumped on his backside by a mere back. It lifted the boys in red and, for the first time, showed a chink of vulnerability in the world champions. My pick at 12, though, goes to Tim Horan. Arguably Walter Little would be a close second, being the often overlooked and under-rated linchpin, the player who put the celebrated talents of Christian Cullen, Lomu and Wilson into space, but Horan, a two-time world champion for Australia and a player with brains, brawn and guile, gets my nod for his all-round ability.

13. Jeremy Guscott

Another player whose confidence and outspokenness rarely invited warmth from others, but he was so innately talented that the game just looked so easy for him. Without a dominant pack or a hard man at 12 you would pick others in his place, but like the magic of the halfbacks, your 13 on occasions needs to be able to cast spells. Jerry had this ability in spades and, aligned to his floating glide, the sign of class is to appear to have time. Whether people waited off him, scared of what he'd do, or allowed him space, wanting him to do it, he always looked as though he was in no hurry.

14. Gerald Davies

Though Lote Tuqiri would be more of a handful in the modern game, this teacher and Cambridge graduate played with the same tempo, poise and poetry with which he now writes. Writing in the build-up to an England–Wales game, marking Shane Williams, I was asked to compare him to the great GD. 'As a child, my father spoke of Gerald and said that he was so fast he could flick the switch on the wall and be in bed before the light went out!' I've tried this on countless occasions, wanting myself to possess the same powers. Thus, 'If Shane can do that I know we're in for a long afternoon!' Gerald Davies is a legend and Shane Williams is a player cast in the same mould – small, dark, quick, extremely popular with Welsh supporters who recognise and appreciate the Celtic flair of one of their very own. Gerald once wrote that 'the sidestep is the small man's retribution', and so it is – what a man!

15. Me!

I'm picking the team, and behind this lot I reckon even I could be made to look half decent.

ALTERNATIVE DREAM XV

1. Winston Churchill

Belligerent, determined, uncompromising.

2. Ernest Shackleton

Not exactly scared of putting his body in harm's way. His jovial humour and positive attitude must have been an absolute godsend on those cold February Tuesday training sessions at, errr ... minus-140 degrees C with only seal blubber to chew on!

3. Toad, from *The Wind in the Willows*

Every team needs an eccentric, exuberant victim. He would be the butt of everyone's jokes and still be the one to laugh last. A child at heart, yet with enormous wealth and power, he could be manipulated to get the best facilities for the squad. Stroppy and moody like all good tight heads, but deep down he had a good heart and was eager to please.

4. Optimus Prime

The biggest of the goodie Transformers. Gentle off the pitch, he can metamorphosise into a huge monster on it.

5. Hagrid

J.K. Rowling's loveable softie. I'll give him the benefit of the doubt knowing that under the Mongol's tutorage a nasty side could be found that could put his eight-foot frame to decent use.

6. Ranulph Fiennes

Talk about mental toughness, doggedness and resilience!

7. Genghis Khan (captain), 'the Wolf of the Plains'

Schooled in the class of warrior wolf kings, uniting and leading an illiterate race to conquer one-third of the globe, compassionate yet ruthless, loved by his kin, he clearly knew a bit about leadership.

8. Darth Vader

The greatest villain in cinematic history and, though few people would know this, he is in fact a Bristolian (my favourite city)!

9. Bruce Lee

Quick hands.

10. Yoda

The magical 'force' is strong with this one. Also, having been exiled by the Galactic Empire, he must have had a bit of 'niggle' about him!

11. Usain Bolt

I like my wingers to have a bit of character about them. This one is tall enough to play in the lineout and, let's face it, you're not going to skin him on the outside.

12. Maximus Decimus Meridius

Took himself quite seriously, but skilful and yet quite nails, really. Rocky would be my crash ball merchant, with the little general being the brains of the midfield operation. Though being the strategist, and having the skills to pay the bills, he wouldn't be scared of doing his share of graft too.

13. Rocky Balboa

All heart. The character whose eponymous film and theme tune inspired a generation to get in shape, whose rags-to-riches story epitomised the American dream that anyone can make it from 'bum' to world champ.

14. Prince Akheem of Zamunda/Billy Ray Valentine

Eddie Murphy's best characters. Chopsey, loud, flash and gregarious. Paul Sackey makes me laugh almost every day doing impressions of them. Eddie Murphy was also a school sprinting champion but he gets the nod for humour alone.

15. David Stirling

Founder of the SAS, 'Who Dares Wins'; the same philosophy is true in sport. Play within your shell, inhibited, and you'll ultimately lose. Brave, tough and intelligent.

Coach: Jeremy Clarkson

Straight-talking, no messing and good for morale.

Medic: Boudicca

Having burned the Romans alive in their temple, she was not renowned for her sympathetic nature. My players would make sure they were fit to train rather than suffer at the hands of her 'tough love'.

Vital Statistics

Name: Owen Joshua Lewsey

Birth: 30 November 1976, Bromley, Kent

Height: 5 ft 11 in (1.8 m)

Weight: 13 st 10 lbs (87 kgs)

CLUB APPEARANCES

SEASON		All games			League			Cup			Europe			CLUB HONOURS
		App	T	Pts	App	T	Pts	App	T	Pts	App	T	Pts	
1995-96	Wasps	3	-	-										
1996-97	Bristol	9+2	2	10	7+1	2	10							
1997-98	Bristol	23+4	-	38	15+2	5	36	1	-	-	5	-	2	
1998-99	Wasps	25	5	25	21	4	20	4	1	5				Tetley's Bitter Cup winners
1999-00	Wasps	28	11	55	18	9	45	4	1	5	6	1	5	Tetley's Bitter Cup winners
2000-01	Wasps	22+2	7	35	15+2	5	25	1	-	-	4	2	10	
2001-02	Wasps	21	4	20	17	2	10	1	-	-	2	1	5	
2002-03	Wasps	28+1	15	75	23+1	12	60	1	-	-	4	3	15	Zurich Premiership champions/Parker Pen Challenge Cup winners
2003-04	Wasps	15+1	5	25	8+1	2	10			7	3	1	5	Heineken Cup winners/Zurich Premiership champions
2004-05	Wasps	19+2	7	35	11+2	4	20	1	1	5	6	2	10	Zurich Premiership champions
2005-06	Wasps	18+2	7	35	9+1	3	15	4+1	1	10	5	2	10	Powergen Cup winners
2006-07	Wasps	23+2	8	40	14+1	3	15	1	1	5	8+1	4	20	Heineken Cup winners
2007-08	Wasps	19+5	5	25	16+2	5	25	1+1	-	-	2+2	-	-	Guinness Premiership champions
2008-09	Wasps	11	2	10	7	-	-	2	1	5	2	1	5	
TOTALS		264+21	79	433	181+13	56	291	21+3	7	35	51+3	19	97	

REPRESENTATIVE MATCHES

Date	Team	Opponent	Venue	Tourny	Res	Shirt	Scoring
08/02/1997	England Under-21	France Under-21	Leicester		L	10	
05/12/1997	England Under-21	Nike NZ Under-21	Newbury		W	16	Drop goal
20/02/1998	England Under-21	Wales Under-21	Worcester		W	15	
20/03/1998	England A	Scotland A	Inverleith		L	18	
03/04/1998	England A	Ireland A	Richmond		W	10	Try
13/06/1998	England XV	New Zealand A	Hamilton		L	10	Conv, Penalty
16/06/1998	England XV	NZ Academy	Invercargill		L	16	
20/06/1998	ENGLAND	New Zealand	Dunedin		L	12	
27/06/1998	ENGLAND	New Zealand	Auckland		L	10	
04/07/1998	ENGLAND	South Africa	Cape Town		L	10	
13/06/2000	England XV	North-West Districts	Potchefstroom		W	17	Try
20/06/2000	England XV	Griqualand West	Kimberley		W	17	
28/06/2000	England XV	Eastern Transvaal	Brakpan		W	15	
26/01/2001	England 7s		Mar del Plata	WC7			
16/02/2001	England A	Italy A	Bedford		W	12	Try
02/03/2001	England A	Scotland A	Leeds		W	15	
06/04/2001	England A	France A	Redruth		W	15	
27/05/2001	England XV	Barbarians	Twickenham		L	12	
02/06/2001	ENGLAND	Canada	Markham		W	15	2 tries

REPRESENTATIVE MATCHES continued

Date	Team	Opponent	Venue	Tourny	Res	Shirt	Scoring
09/06/2001	ENGLAND	Canada	Burnaby Lake		W	15	
16/06/2001	ENGLAND	United States	San Francisco		W	15	2 tries
04/01/2002	England 7s		Santiago	WSS			
11/01/2002	England 7s		Mar del Plata	WSS			
01/02/2002	England A	Scotland A	Stirling		D	15	
15/02/2002	England A	Ireland A	Northampton		L	11	
01/03/2002	England A	France A	Limoges		L	12	
17/03/2002	England 7s		Beijing	WSS			
22/03/2002	England 7s		Hong Kong	WSS			
24/05/2002	England 7s		Twickenham	WSS			
02/08/2002	England 7s		Manchester	CG7			
14/02/2003	England A	France A	Northampton		W	15	
09/03/2003	ENGLAND	Italy	Twickenham	6NC	W	15	2 tries
22/03/2003	ENGLAND	Scotland	Twickenham	6NC	W	15	Try
30/03/2003	ENGLAND	Ireland	Lansdowne Road	6NC	W	15	
14/06/2003	ENGLAND	New Zealand	Wellington		W	15	
21/06/2003	ENGLAND	Australia	Melbourne		W	15	
30/08/2003	ENGLAND	France	Marseille		L	14	
06/09/2003	ENGLAND	France	Twickenham		W	22	Try

Date	Team	Opponent	Venue	Competition	Result		Notes
12/10/2003	ENGLAND	Georgia	Perth	RWC	W	15	
18/10/2003	ENGLAND	South Africa	Perth	RWC	W	15	
02/11/2003	ENGLAND	Uruguay	Brisbane	RWC	W	15	5 tries
16/11/2003	ENGLAND	France	Sydney	RWC	W	15	
22/11/2003	ENGLAND	Australia	Sydney	RWC	W	15	
15/02/2004	ENGLAND	Italy	Rome	6NC	W	14	Try
21/02/2004	ENGLAND	Scotland	Murrayfield	6NC	W	14	Try
06/03/2004	ENGLAND	Ireland	Twickenham	6NC	L	14	
20/03/2004	ENGLAND	Wales	Twickenham	6NC	W	14	
27/03/2004	ENGLAND	France	Stade de France	6NC	L	14	Try
12/06/2004	ENGLAND	New Zealand	Dunedin		L	15	
19/06/2004	ENGLAND	New Zealand	Auckland		L	15	
26/06/2004	ENGLAND	Australia	Brisbane		L	15	
13/11/2004	ENGLAND	Canada	Twickenham		W	11	2 tries
20/11/2004	ENGLAND	South Africa	Twickenham		W	11	
27/11/2004	ENGLAND	Australia	Twickenham		L	11	Try
05/02/2005	ENGLAND	Wales	Cardiff	6NC	L	11	
13/02/2005	ENGLAND	France	Twickenham	6NC	L	11	Try
27/02/2005	ENGLAND	Ireland	Lansdowne Road	6NC	L	11	
12/03/2005	ENGLAND	Italy	Twickenham	6NC	W	11	
19/03/2005	ENGLAND	Scotland	Twickenham	6NC	W	11	Try
04/06/2005	British Isles XV	Bay of Plenty	Rotorua		W	15	2 tries
11/06/2005	British Isles XV	NZ Maori	Hamilton		L	15	

REPRESENTATIVE MATCHES continued

Date	Team	Opponent	Venue	Tourny	Res	Shirt	Scoring
15/06/2005	British Isles XV	Wellington Lions	Wellington		W	15	
25/06/2005	BRITISH & IRISH LIONS	New Zealand	Christchurch		L	14	
02/07/2005	BRITISH & IRISH LIONS	New Zealand	Wellington		L	15	
09/07/2005	BRITISH & IRISH LIONS	New Zealand	Auckland		L	11	
12/11/2005	ENGLAND	Australia	Twickenham		W	15	
19/11/2005	ENGLAND	New Zealand	Twickenham		L	15	
26/11/2005	ENGLAND	Samoa	Twickenham		W	15	
04/02/2006	ENGLAND	Wales	Twickenham	6NC	W	15	
25/02/2006	ENGLAND	Scotland	Murrayfield	6NC	L	15	
12/03/2006	ENGLAND	France	Stade de France	6NC	L	15	
11/11/2006	ENGLAND	Argentina	Twickenham	L	22		
18/11/2006	ENGLAND	South Africa	Twickenham		W	15	
25/11/2006	ENGLAND	South Africa	Twickenham		L	15	
03/02/2007	ENGLAND	Scotland	Twickenham	6NC	W	14	
10/02/2007	ENGLAND	Italy	Twickenham	6NC	W	14	
24/02/2007	ENGLAND	Ireland	Croke Park	6NC	L	14	
11/03/2007	ENGLAND	France	Twickenham	6NC	W	15	
11/08/2007	ENGLAND	France	Twickenham		L	11	
18/08/2007	ENGLAND	France	Marseille		L	14	

Date	Team	Opponent	Venue	Tournament	Result		Try
08/09/2007	ENGLAND	United States	Lens	RWC	W	14	
14/09/2007	ENGLAND	South Africa	Stade de France	RWC	L	14	
22/09/2007	ENGLAND	Samoa	Nantes	RWC	W	15	
28/09/2007	ENGLAND	Tonga	Parc des Princes	RWC	W	15	
06/10/2007	ENGLAND	Australia	Marseille	RWC	W	11	
13/10/2007	ENGLAND	France	Stade de France	RWC	W	11	Try

Tournament Key

RWC – Rugby World Cup, WC7 – World Cup Sevens, CG7 – Commonwealth Games 7s, WSS – IRB World Sevens Series, 6NC – Six Nations Championship

Acknowledgements

I'd like to thank everyone who's helped me compile this book especially Ed, Davina, Sophia and Toby at Virgin. Special mention must go to my old chum, Humfrey.

Thanks and apologies to my teammates and roommates. I know that I've kept to myself during these months of writing the book – but perhaps that's been a blessing in disguise!

Finally, thanks to my old schoolteacher John Williams, who, before every international game or final, never fails to send me a kind message of support and advice. Thank you, John, your words have meant a lot to me and are much appreciated.

Index

JL indicates Josh Lewsey.